Revised Edition $1.25

IF YOU MARRY OUTSIDE YOUR FAITH

Counsel on Mixed Marriages

BY JAMES A. PIKE

IF YOU MARRY OUTSIDE YOUR FAITH

IF YOU MARRY

OUTSIDE

YOUR FAITH

Counsel on Mixed Marriages

JAMES A. PIKE

REVISED EDITION

HARPER & ROW, PUBLISHERS

New York and Evanston

IF YOU MARRY OUTSIDE YOUR FAITH

Revised Edition

Library of Congress catalog card number: 62-11135

To My Children

Catherine Hope
James Albert

Constance Ann
Christopher

CONTENTS

PREFACE

A successful marriage does not just come naturally. From the day John and Mary meet till the day they are separated by death each remains a separate personality—each with a unique make-up and each with a will of his own. No harmony achieved is ever static. The "changes and chances of this mortal life" are such that the tune is never the same and hence new harmonizations are always called for if discords are to be avoided.

Conscious concern for harmony is of course important, but even more important are the unconscious influences which shape the two lives. Social and family influences are important but they are unreliable: they represent "every wind of doctrine" and they rarely nourish and heal the inner man, especially when there are feelings of inadequacy, failure, temptation, guilt, indecision, insecurity; nor are they likely to insure common reactions to the problems and claims a couple must face. The richest source of inspiration and insight, trust and hope is found in religious conviction and devotion. This is true of the individual; but it is even more essential in the lives of those who, though two, are to live as one.

And there are parentheses in the course of romantic love—in any marriage. If these gaps are to be bridged, and thus the stability of the union be maintained until natural love returns, a reliable resource for love and concern beyond each other's whims or words is a prime requisite. Hence the importance in a marriage of a continuous experience of the love of God—a love which does not depend upon our lovableness but upon our need of love. Such a love is both a model and a source of the bond of love that remains alive in a marriage in those times when all else fails, and all the while nourishes the natural love of each beloved for the other.

A person's religion is his framework of meaning, the source of his priority scale of values, the measure of his hopes, the well spring of his most secure joys. When two people decide for a lifetime to pool their strengths and weaknesses, their hopes and fears, the religious dimension in the personality of each of necessity plays its part—consciously or unconsciously—in their most significant relationships, decisions and responses to each other. Lacks, conflicts or closed doors in the matter of religion cannot be brushed aside as a mere matter of the private taste of each party.

The author's particular assignments in the ministry have been such that counseling has played a large part in it. As a result he has talked to a great number of people about marriage—before, during and after. In this field he has yet to deal with a problem or discern a solution which was not at root religious. And he has observed that an initial diversity of religious faith, which may at the outset present more difficulty than a more homogeneous situation, has at least the advantage of bringing the matter of religion in the marriage to the fore, with the result that if a solution is found the marriage is usually better grounded religiously than where the couple has not been forced to take so seriously the spiritual aspect of their union.

Thus it is on a positive and hopeful note that he here approaches a subject that can seem so distressing to those personally confronted with it. For their sakes it is important that the treatment be as honest and realistic as possible; hence actual cases with which the author has dealt are utilized throughout the book, with appropriate alteration of names and details in order to preserve anonymity. To these counselees must go my first acknowledgment of thanks: to them, especially the many who had the courage to carry through with the logical implications of the problem, I principally owe any confidence I have as to the analysis herein.

I wish, too, to express my appreciation to Mr. Wilfred E. Boughton and Mrs. Catherine M. Morton, who assisted in the collection of materials in Chapters VI and VII and typed the manuscript.

It is appropriate to record appreciation to my wife, who not only read the manuscript critically, but contributed to one of the main theses of this book in that it was together we came to serious religious faith after our marriage. I have dedicated the book to our four children: though their charming distractiveness did not always contribute to the progress of the writing, they represented throughout a very tangible image of one of the main reasons for religious unity in a home, and also their multiple presence freed me from any implication that the position taken in Chapter III might be self-serving.

I can wish no more for those who seek help herein than that their marriages will be as blessed as ours has been.

PREFACE TO THE SECOND EDITION

There are two reasons for this revision:

1. Since the publication of the first edition, there have been additional statements of position on the subject matter by national Church bodies, and additional court cases of interest.

2. In my continued counseling in this field some new insights have come and I have also profited by readers' comments on various points, and thus have seen the need of clarification or expansion of the text in a number of places.

I am therefore grateful that the publishers have permitted me not only to add certain material to "up-date" the book, but also to undertake a thorough revision of the entire text.

I hope that the fact of the book's revision will increase what I have been led to understand is its helpfulness in what is an increasing area of pastoral concern.

✠James A. Pike

The Cathedral Close
San Francisco, California

IF YOU MARRY OUTSIDE YOUR FAITH

CHAPTER I

❧❧

WHY THIS BOOK IS WRITTEN

Fifty years ago it would not have been particularly important that any such book as this be written. And if it had been written there would have been few readers because there were few mixed marriages, and few people contemplating such a possibility. But now the mixed marriage is one of the most common phenomena of our time. There are a very large number of people involved, in one way or another, in the problem this type of marriage presents.

Why the change in the situation? Fifty years ago most Roman Catholics in this country were representatives of one of a number of immigrant groups which were definitely marked off from their neighbors in terms of means, education, economic opportunity and cultural advantage. The Jews in America by and large were still in a religious and cultural ghetto. Atheists and agnostics there were, but there was little understanding then about the significance of secularism and its bearing upon life attitudes; it was more or less assumed that one really was what one was christened or that he would sooner or later fit in with the proper religious formalities in a sort of "Life with Father" fashion. Of course always a small minority of the population represented the exception to any of these generalizations. But their existence and their acceptance by the dominant group did not account for a large number of mixed marriages.

WHY MIXED MARRIAGES USED TO BE RARER

Those who themselves put religion first in life would of course like to think that the relative rarity of mixed marriages in those days had to do with religious conviction on the part of people. This may be partially the case, but to assume that it explains the situation is a bit naïve. The basis of barriers was oftentimes somewhat less spiritual. The fact is that the people of Anglo-Saxon stock (and certain other older groups, such as the very early Dutch and German immigrants) had arrived here first, had gotten hold of the best lands, developed a working capital, and thus had in hand more of "what it takes." This advantage enabled them to become better educated and to provide better education for their children. It enabled them to provide more comfortable surroundings and wider opportunities for leisure—and hence for culture. Further, the economic structure of the time—without the interference of income tax and its wealth-distributing corollaries—left a great gap between the "ins" and "outs." Thus the opportunity of social contact between them was markedly low and when contact was made it was sufficiently suggestive—or even scandalous—to form what became a standard plot for the American novel and drama. As a matter of fact even those who would enjoy (and feel democratic about enjoying) the presentation of such Cinderella stories, found themselves personally upset at the enactment of these scenes in their own families and by their own kith and kin.

And the barrier was not entirely economic. Even as between the members of two immigrant groups, the process of assimilation, the working of the melting pot, was so insufficiently advanced that the opportunities for social contacts were few and the chances of intermarriage were reduced, even among members of the same religious groups. To this day there are some remnants of the prejudice as to the marriages of Irish and Italians—even though usually no religious problem is presented. And there are still remnants today of the prejudice—

on both sides—against the intermarriage of German and Polish or Russian Jews, though again no religious problem is necessarily presented.

WHY THEY ARE MORE COMMON TODAY

Things are quite different today. Except for the existence of enclaves in our larger urban centers, by and large the process of assimilation is well advanced. Second- and third-generation Irish, Jewish and Italian families have had widespread economic and educational opportunities. Jews graduate from Harvard and gentiles with generations of Anglo-Saxon background graduate from the Upland State Teachers College. Roman Catholics belong to the best clubs, clubs to which many of old English stock cannot get admitted. Suburbia shelters side by side people of all backgrounds and religions.

There are at least three other factors at work which make the matter of mixed marriages a more pressing problem. After a long dry spell in which religious indifferentism was the mode, people are once again taking religion more seriously and noting its bearing upon everyday life, especially in the marriage relationship. Protestants are certainly more religiously self-conscious—and many are more denominationally self-conscious—than they were a generation ago. And the last twenty years has seen Roman Catholicism take on a more aggressive character in America, and that as a result of the new station it has in our common life, both in terms of numbers and in the affluence and education of its members.

Further, a new complication has arisen. The line between the believer and the unbeliever is now more sharp. The unbeliever has less of a residual religious culture, operates less on an ethic inherited from a grandfather who believed in—and feared—God. The believer, on the other hand, is more aware of his difference from those who do not care for religion. The religious folk—while part of a now rapidly growing movement, are now more conscious of themselves as minority groups and thus are more likely to be wedded to the way of life which their particular religious faith implies.

The final factor is the degree to which marriage in general has been failing. It used to be assumed that any couple who got married—whatever the circumstances—were apt to stay married. Now this is not assumed at all, particularly where there is a state in which the divorce rate is 50 per cent of the marriage rate, and in a see city where it is 55 per cent. And hence many people are much more concerned with insuring in advance those circumstances which will make it more likely that the particular marriage may escape defeat.

THE IGNORANCE AND CONFUSION ON THE SUBJECT

But now at the very time that this issue has become so obvious, there is a widespread ignorance of the basic facts and ideas which are involved. While the Roman Catholic attitude on this subject is quite generally known, at least in rough outline, it is widely misunderstood, and there are few subjects on which others are more prejudiced. On the other hand, the Roman Catholics have practically no knowledge of the official attitude of other religious groups on this subject. For this they are not entirely to be blamed, because most Protestants, for example, are unaware of the specific attitudes of their own churches or of the principles which should underlie any decision they are called upon to make in the premises. And when there is a knowledge of the problem in terms of the barriers which it presents, there is not equally a constructive view toward the positive aspect of the relation of religion to marriage.

Case 1. Mary is explaining her problem to her mother: "Of course, I would like to be married by our own minister; but you see, since John is a Roman Catholic, we must be married by a priest. His church has a rule on this subject and under this rule I have to promise that the children will be raised Roman Catholic. Of course I don't like it; but his church has a rule and ours doesn't, and so the only way we can get married is for me to give in." Mary's mother says: "I think that is too bad; because we have been Presbyterians for many generations. But I guess nothing can be done about it." "No," says Mary, "John says nothing can be."

Actually this whole line is incorrect. It so happens that the Presbyterian Church does have a position on the matter,[1] and even if it didn't, it affirms an ethical system which has definite implications related to this subject.[2] If Mary in full knowledge of all this decided to yield to John, that is one thing. But it is unfortunate that time and time again non-Roman parties yield on the false assumption that only one church has any concern about the matter or has any position on the subject.

Case 2. Albert's father is expressing to his wife his reaction to the antenuptial agreement proposed by the Roman Catholic Church: "I think it is very un-American and undemocratic. Why should they have the right to tell my son what religion his children are to be raised in? Besides, for them to say that the marriage wouldn't be valid if they were married in the Methodist Church is to say, dear, that you and I aren't married because we were married by a Methodist minister."

The first part of this comment is irrelevant; there is no denial of Albert's religious freedom: Albert doesn't have to marry the Roman Catholic girl at all. In fact it would be the denial of the religious freedom of any group to say that it could not lay down conditions for its own members as to the conduct of their lives. (Some very Protestant religious groups, for example, lay down the rule that there is to be no drinking in the home.) As to the second part of the comment, the Roman Catholic Church does not in fact question the validity of a marriage of two baptized persons if neither has ever been a Roman Catholic.

[1] See pp. 80–82 below.
[2] See ch. VI, below.

These two illustrations will suffice to suggest the ignorance and confusion that is widespread on this subject. Even with all the facts and with a full understanding of the issues at stake—from both points of view—the problem is difficult enough. But it is made much more difficult and produces more tension when the parties involved and their relatives and friends are operating on false premises. By and large, American people do not know enough about this problem and an increasing number of the American people are being faced with it.

THE APPROACH TO BE USED

That is why this book is written. No book, no matter how clearly written, can compel a right course of action; as a matter of fact, the approach taken by this book will be such that it may for some make the decision as to the right course of action a more complicated one—for here we are going to avoid all oversimplifications and try to smoke out clichés and prejudices which cause people to make snap judgments. But any couple which enters into a mixed marriage, no matter how simple their naïveté may have allowed the subject to appear at the time they were married, will sooner or later run into all the complications which in fact exist. It is our belief that it is better to face these complications beforehand, even if so doing somewhat muddies the waters of romance.

On the other hand, problems which the couples themselves have thought were hopeless can, by a right understanding of the issues, and through the help of the right kind of counsel and prayerful thought, reach a happy solution. The author has, in fact, used the approach which will be outlined in this book with scores of couples and more often than not a happy outcome has been achieved. But generally the outcome has come after a period of travail in which the barriers were made even more evident through realistic analysis. The difference between the approach we will take here and the more naïve one is a difference between the honest physician who says to a sick patient: "You are really sick; here is what the trouble is. If you take this medicine you will probably get well," and one who says: "You are really not sick. I just wouldn't think about it any more; go on living your life." The latter is immediately more satisfying; but the former may lead to a real cure. I will thus take the liberty of asking the reader, in fairness to his own situation and to the author, to read the entire book, and not be too discouraged by the realistic analysis in the early chapters. The solutions suggested will be meaningful only after the problem has been seen in correct perspective.

"TO WHOM IT MAY CONCERN"

This book is intended for a number of types of readers:

1. Those who are personally faced with decisions in regard to their own marriages.

2. Those who already are partners to a mixed marriage and are having difficulties which were not fully taken into account during their courtship.

3. Parents, relatives and friends who find themselves called upon to give helpful advice or who are emotionally involved in the contemplated marriage of their loved ones.

4. Those whose business it is to counsel people in difficulty and who often run up against this particular difficulty; priests, ministers, and rabbis; school and college counselors; and the like.

5. The general reader, since this is an increasingly important phenomenon in our culture: to relieve prejudices and to sharpen proper convictions.

A word about these last two phrases: at first blush they would seem to be inconsistent. It has long been a myth in American culture that having firm religious convictions increases religious prejudice. Actually this is not the case in these simple terms. A religious conviction based on ignorance, or without knowledge of alternatives, or without mature analysis of the premises upon which the conviction rests, can increase religious prejudice, as the whole history of mankind has shown. But a religious conviction based on a free choice among alternatives, when one's own views and others have been thoughtfully considered, need not be a cause of prejudice; in fact one who has gone through this very process in an adult way is most likely to be sympathetic and understanding toward the views of others and toward the decisions which they have felt they must make on their own premises. How in practice this process works out in this particular field will be seen as we go along.

CHAPTER II

THE MIXED MARRIAGE
IN OPERATION

M OST PEOPLE THINK of the problem as "antenuptial." They think of it as a clumsy predicament imposed upon a young couple in love by organized religion, by denominational differences. It is generally assumed that if these problems can be surmounted one way or another, if some *modus operandi* can be devised or—quite simply—if one party or the other will yield, then the couple will live their married life as any couple who did not have the problem to solve in the first place. Thus the question is often posed this way: "If only your church didn't take the view that it does . . ." or "If you simply go ahead and sign the papers, dear, everything will be all right." But, as we shall see, the reason that organized religion does create the antenuptial problems, and at least one or two groups require antenuptial contracts, is that there is a problem in the marriage itself. Thus we will make better sense out of the premarital problem if we will examine a little more closely the married life of persons of different religious persuasion.

THE FALLACY OF THE ISOLATED ILLUSTRATION

Here we must be realistic, because this matter is usually bypassed by some such remark as "Aunt Minnie and Uncle Joe have had no trouble; they simply agreed to disagree and in fact are one of the happiest couples I know." Anyone can readily find some couple of his acquaintance who will serve as the model for such a comment.

Now to get the problem of this chapter focused, the author is prepared to say at the outset that Aunt Minnie's and Uncle Joe's marriage is *not* an ideal one and a great deal that is important is lacking. He would say this regardless of what names were substituted for Aunt Minnie and for Uncle Joe. We will see a little later on why I make such a categorical statement. Meanwhile let us assume for a moment that the particular marriage given as an illustration is an exemplary one in every way, that it represents all that could ever be desired in married life. That still doesn't answer the question as to whether John and Mary, of different religious faiths, now contemplating marriage, should enter a mixed marriage.

When something has already happened we can hope that it works out well; but in our decisions about future matters, we do not generally base our decisions upon isolated instances, but upon calculated risks based upon statistical averages. Suppose you wanted to fly the Atlantic and asked the agent: "Is it a safe trip?" and he answered: "Oh yes; every once in a while a plane gets through," I doubt if you would book passage. What you would want to know—if you still had the courage to pursue the matter further—is, What are the chances? What is important to a young couple contemplating the matter is not that this or that couple seem to have worked it out all right, but rather, What by and large is the success of mixed marriages? Fortunately this is a question we are able to answer—in a rough and ready way to be sure, because the answer is in terms of divorce and separation—which is only a partial reflection of the scope of unhappiness and dissatisfaction which it suggests.

WHAT THE FIGURES SHOW

From what is called the "Maryland Study" we learn about the religious connection of the parents of twelve thousand young people, and whether their parents were living together or not. The study was sponsored by the American Council on Education with the title "Youth Tell Their Story," and with Dr. Howard M. Bell as the author and compiler. The figures show that where both parents were Protestants (using this word in its customary broad sense) 6.8 per cent of the parents were separated. (This and all the other figures would have of course been higher were not childless marriages excluded by the nature of the study.) Where both parents were Roman Catholic 6.4 per cent of the parents were separated. In the case of mixed marriages 15.2 per cent represented broken homes (it is interesting for us to note in connection with the discussion later on that where the parents had no religion 16.7 per cent of the homes were broken—the largest of all categories). In short there was in the case of mixed marriages 2¼ times as much separation and divorce as in the familes where there was religious homogeneity.[1] With one out of four or five marriages reaching the courts these days, this differential of 2¼ to 1 as to the chance of success is not an unimportant consideration! It is not enough to say at this point, "Oh well, ours wouldn't work out that way, because we are in love." It may reasonably be assumed that 90 per cent of all couples involved in the statistical study started out with this conviction or some reasonable facsimile of it. These statistics perhaps supply the reason why in a recent poll 75 per cent of the Protestants asked were opposed to mixed marriages, though it leaves one surprised that only 54 per cent of the Roman Catholics asked registered objection.[2]

Back to Aunt Minnie and Uncle Joe. There is another difficulty in using a single illustration of this sort. The real question is not are Aunt Minnie and Uncle Joe happier in their religiously hybrid state than Aunt Nellie and Uncle Frank who are of the same faith. The real questions are: How

---

[1] Even greater disparity is shown by Washington and Michigan studies. *Social Forces*, XXI, 334 (1943); *American Sociological Review*, XIV, 401 (1949). Cf. the analysis in Bossard and Boll, *One Marriage, Two Faiths* (Ronald Press, 1957).

[2] Survey conducted by *The New World*, published by the Roman Catholic Archdiocese of Chicago. *New York Times*, July 18, 1953.

much worse off would the latter marriage be if they didn't have the tie of common religious faith? and, How much better off would the former marriage be if, in addition to whatever natural factors contribute to a good marriage, they had the undergirding support of a common religious allegiance? This is the only sensible comparison—and this is the comparison for the making of which we are rarely in the possession of enough facts.

And there is another "sleeper" in the solution of one's own marriage problem by reference to an isolated example of someone else's marriage. From the outside looking in we can't really know how successful a marriage is. We have all had the experience of greeting the news of a marital breakup with these words: "I never thought it would happen to them; they seemed so happy!" Who knows? The best we can do is to analyze the factors which would seem to provide the most fruitful bases for a happy married life, and in the case of mixed marriages some of these important bases are not there. Let us turn to these underlying factors.

SILENCE IS NO SOLUTION

It is commonly assumed that the main problem which would exist in the mixed marriage is constant quarreling over religion. When a couple are on the brink of such a marriage they can easily convince themselves that they could resolve not to allow such to occur. This they can do—and they can probably keep their resolve. But this does not touch the real problem. Quarreling over religion at least keeps religion to the forefront of the marriage; but a studied silence about it month after month, year after year, means that the religion of either party is for practical purposes not an operative fact in the common development of the married life. This is where the figures provided by the Maryland Study about marriages in which there is no religion at all throws an interesting light on the mixed marriage problem—one in which most people think there is *too much* religion involved. It is interesting to note that the figure reflecting failure in mixed marriages and that reflecting failure in irreligious marriages are about the same. In this connection it is also interesting to turn to Professor Kinsey's tables (in his two studies of sexual behavior) on the relation of adultery to religion in the family. There we see that adultery is about two to one in the case of a marriage without religion. Now it is true that adultery and marital breakup are not quite the same thing; but one need not labor the point that there is a very significant connection between them. The trouble in a marriage without religion and in a mixed marriage—and this they share in common—is that no formal religion plays a significant part in the common life which the couple live together. In each case the couple have no agreed-upon beliefs openly referred to as a basis for decisions, for value judgments, for choices between priorities, for reactions to situations.

THE EFFECT OF RELIGIOUS DIFFERENCES ON OUTLOOK

Speaking quite broadly, a person standing consciously in the Judaeo-Christian tradition, and submitting himself by regular worship to its unconscious influences, looks at life differently than an agnostic does. This is not to indulge in the oversimplification that the former person always does the fine, high-minded thing while the latter person always does an evil, shabby thing. Not at all; but in deciding for good and evil the basis is different in evaluating things—no matter how often the same decision might be reached in particular instances—by those standing within the two world views. Likewise the Roman Catholic and the Methodist, the Episcopalian and the Baptist get at things in different ways. There are certain specific problems which we shall discuss later, such as the matter of contraception, in which there are radically different answers resulting from radically different views of human nature and destiny; but no less important are the divergences in the day-to-day outlook which grow out of differences in personality and make-up which have been shaped and formed by varying religious influences. For example, none would dispute that the conscious and unconscious attitudes toward sex play a large part in proper marital adjustment. Yet the theology and ethics of sex vary greatly in the case of a Roman Catholic, an Episcopalian and a Southern Baptist. We will have a chance as we go along to study other illustrations of the problem.

Case 3. Ann has been taught all her life that drinking is sinful. It formed a frequent subject for the homiletic efforts of her Baptist minister. Her husband, Bill, is a loyal churchman, but being an Episcopalian, he has never in his whole life heard a sermon of this type, and in fact has often enjoyed a glass of beer in the rectory and seen his rector gladly accept an old-fashioned when offered to him. Not only does Ann not join Bill in a drink but always discounts the significance of his own religious life because he both drinks and goes to church: she cannot see how it can be other than hypocritical. She has learned to say nothing about the matter and since Bill never has too much to drink she is not given the opportunity of providing object lessons for her views. This fact in itself is all the more disturbing as it makes her unconsciously uneasy about her own position taken by the Baptist Church, which she still attends.

Case 4. The same facts, except that Ann first had the desire to be agreeable, and later she actually came to enjoy a cocktail before dinner, and now shares her husband's "vice." Since she still continues her old religious allegiances, she feels guilty underneath about the whole matter. This sense of guilt is not too successfully suppressed and expresses itself in ways which on the conscious level seem unrelated; for example, of the two, she is the one more likely to have too much.

Case 5. Before she was married Eileen was a fairly independent-minded Roman Catholic. She was frankly critical of the Roman Catholic domination of the politics—

which happened to be corrupt—in her home city; she did not approve of Franco's side in the Spanish Civil War, etc. She is married to a Congregationalist who is vitally concerned with public issues and who is quite outspoken in his criticism of Roman Catholic attitudes in this field. Eileen now finds herself rushing to the defense of the Roman Catholic Church at all points because she cannot help but interpret (and perhaps rightly) that her husband's sharp criticism of Roman Catholic political attitudes is meant as a criticism of her religion.

Case 6. Kate, a Roman Catholic, tells her husband that she has about decided to select Dr. Murphy as her obstetrician. "But," says her husband, "he is a Catholic. I haven't any doubt that you'll come through all right, but still if serious trouble developed I wouldn't want you to have a doctor who would put the life of the baby ahead of yours. You come first with me!" Kate, concerned about this very question herself (because she hasn't been having an easy time of her pregnancy), is put in the embarrassing position of relaxing her loyalty to her own Church and its teaching if she decides to go to Dr. Stone, who is a prominent Disciple and who at a recent meeting of the county medical association expressed publicly his disdain of the Roman Catholic position on this matter.

Case 7. Yvonne, who has been an agnostic since college days, is very pleased that her daughter has been invited to the birthday party of a schoolmate in a very fashionable family. However, the party conflicts with the closing session of the confirmation class and the husband, a devout Lutheran, has tried to make clear to his daughter the primary importance of her religious obligations over her social obligations. The child herself is torn; and the parents are at odds over the relative value of the two occasions.

Case 8. David, an agnostic Jew, and Marie, a Roman Catholic, are trying to decide on a school for their daughter approaching high school. David is delighted to learn that she can be admitted to Treasdale, which has a very fine scholastic standing and graduation from which almost insures admittance to a good women's college. Marie feels on the other hand that it would be better for her daughter to go to Mount St. Joseph's, especially since Treasdale has been very much influenced by a headmaster who is one of the leaders of the Ethical Culture Society.

In none of these illustrations are we interested in providing the "right" answers. The point is that for the couples involved there are no right answers, because they are looking at each of the questions from quite different perspectives; one may give in or the other may give in; or some sort of working compromise may be achieved. But obviously, in each case, something important is lacking in the marriage: a common world view, a common set of premises from which attitudes are developed and from which, ultimately, decisions of significance are made. In all of these illustrations, whatever the attitude, damage is done to the deepest phases of the life of one of the spouses—in some cases, of both.

DAY IN AND DAY OUT

Entirely apart from crises and big decisions, there is the day-to-day life of the couple. If one of the parties takes his or her religion seriously his conversation would normally reflect it, his outside activities would be, in part at least, connected with the Church, and the deepest moments of his existence would be connected with his faith. For a Jew there are high Holy Days, for a Christian the great festivals. Receiving Holy Communion, worshipping at the crèche, hearing a great and inspiring sermon, bringing another to religious belief—all of these experiences are of the utmost significance to the religious person. When they cannot be shared, when they are ignored or at best can only be greeted with the patronizing interest of an "outsider," there is something devastatingly chilling about the experience of their narration. From day to day, throughout the months and years, a large area of what a marriage can afford is blocked off. Not often does the difference of interest focus itself all in one incident. But a case like the following serves to illustrate boldly what, in the smaller things that make up the ordinary individual's religious life, can become a deep-seated hurt.

Case 9. Mimi had a bad experience with religion as a child and accepted readily the deprecating comments of her college professors against her religion, but decided that she could "tolerate" the religious concern of her fiancé. He was an accountant when she married him but three years later he announced to her that as a result of a long period of thought and prayer he had decided to go into the ministry. She had gloried in his financial success and professional prestige and did not have the resources to enter with enthusiasm into his new decision.

This may not seem a very common possibility, and yet such things are more common these days than heretofore. In any case it focuses what in smaller ways is constantly happening in such a marriage. One of the most important aspects of a marriage is the capacity to enter enthusiastically into the concerns of the spouse—to enter them from the inside, not merely from the outside. When this is lacking a great deal is lacking.

On the whole we have been dealing with the negative aspects of the matter. Actually the reaction of a spouse may be more vigorous, and he may with difficulty suppress his feelings.

Case 10. Teresa has just finished a novena during which she has been to church for nine evenings while her husband has filled in his time as best he can. He has been "out with the boys" some, he has stayed home and read some, and taken comfort from his pipe and a bottle of Scotch. She has had a great religious experience from the novena and has arrived home with a medal that she had purchased and had blessed by one of the priests. He asked casually (as he said later; but actually he wasn't so casual, since this medal became the focus of nine days of resentment), "What is *that?*" Teresa had generally been more cautious, but she was feeling quite inspired with the whole week's experience (she had also been to Communion every morning) and so she said, "It is a scapular of Our Lady of Mount Carmel, and if I keep certain conditions it carries with it the 'sabbatine privilege.'" "What's that?" he asked. "That means that the first Saturday after I am in Purgatory Our Blessed Mother will come and release me." Not knowing quite what to say, he said, "Oh, that's rather long-range planning on your part, I would say!" Then he bit his tongue because he knew he had said the wrong thing; he had not really known quite what to say. There wasn't much useful conversation the rest of the evening.

"LOOKING DOWN ONE'S NOSE" AT THE OTHER'S RELIGION

Even more complicated psychologically is the fact that in a mixed marriage one of the Churches often takes a "Jim Crow" attitude toward the other, and there is a resultant psychological "kick-back" on the part of the party put in this position. Often the emancipated unbeliever will feel superior in his degree of sophistication to the pious partner and, if the latter is unable to make a very good case for views nevertheless tenaciously held, their mutual interplay of resentment can run deep and affect all the other relationships. Where one partner is a Biblical fundamentalist and a rigorist in his attitude toward the joys of life, he is apt to look with scorn upon the liberal religion of his Congregationalist or Episcopal spouse— a scorn heightened sometimes by a submerged "inferiority complex" as to the beauty of building and cult and the educational level of the adherents in the church of his partner. The latter, on the other hand, is likely to regard his spouse as "dogmatic" and at the same time have a hidden suspicion that the spouse is more "religious."

But the "Jim Crow" situation is most marked where one of the parties is a Roman Catholic and where the other party has complied with the demands of the Roman Catholic Church about the "promises." The fact that in the eyes of one of the parties and of his Church the marriage would not have been valid if performed by the minister of the other party's Church, and the fact that it is agreed in advance that the children are to be raised in the Roman Catholic faith, themselves represent claims upon the part of the Roman Catholic party that his faith is the superior of the two. But this is not the whole picture.

The fact that the other party was willing to consent to the arrangement and give up his prospective children to the Roman Catholic Church is living evidence of the fact that he did not take his religious affiliation as seriously as did the Roman Catholic party and did not regard it as worthy of a claim upon him, nor a heritage worth preserving for his children. While the Roman Catholic party naturally welcomed the concession upon the part of the other spouse that enabled him to be married in a way which keeps him in good standing in his own Church, nevertheless this very concession supplies the basis for a contempt for the other partner's religion, for a religion that could be so lightly viewed, for a Church that he —and the other party for that matter—assumes has no serious stake in the matter one way or the other. It thus may seem to both parties that the non-Roman Catholic party has a "second-rate" religion.

This is reinforced by the teaching of the Roman Catholic Church that other "Churches" are not part of the Christian Church—in fact are not Churches at all and that the members of the same, if they are saved at all, are saved because of their "invincible ignorance" (none too flattering a designation) of the claims of the Roman Catholic, the "true" Church. Well-meaning attempts of the Roman Catholic party to ease the situation all too often have a patronizing air. This "down-grading" of the other party's Church becomes even more evident when the children enter the picture. The children trot off with the Roman Catholic party to Mass and are not permitted to share with the other spouse in his religious interests or affiliations. As they grow older they are taught explicitly that the religion of one of their parents is heretical, that his Church is no Church. Human nature is all too susceptible to possible bases of superiority over other people and since a sincere Roman Catholic believes that religion is the most important aspect of life, the downgrading of the other party in this regard often results in a downgrading of his attitudes and views in other respects and the other party often ends up being a second-class citizen in his own household. The reaction can take any form from the explicit "because you are not a Catholic you wouldn't understand" to ill-concealed emphases in conversation, to unconscious factors in the attitude of the Roman Catholic members of the family to the religious outsider.

Of course on the other side of the matter, in spite of the greatest objectivity and tact, the other party is bound to react in ways unfavorable to the peace and stability of the marriage. His only protection against the sense of superiority of a Roman Catholic spouse and children is a contempt for Roman Catholic practices and a distrust of the Roman Catholic Church. The more such an attitude is suppressed the more exaggerated and unreasonable it can become. Even if he expresses a perfectly normal reaction that a Roman Catholic might express, such as, "I really don't like Father McCarthy," it is taken for prejudice on his part (which it well may be) and if he expresses his views on various aspects of Roman Catholic teaching and practice (which normally in a household one would feel free to do) the Roman Catholic party feels he is being untrue to his promise not to try to influence the other or to interfere with the Roman Catholic upbringing of the children. In other words, even the critical spirit which might receive its natural expression in a fully Roman Catholic household (because not all Roman Catholics by any means like everything about their own Church, its policies or personnel) now becomes a source of touchiness, even a symbol of marital disloyalty.

WHAT THIS AMBIVALENCE DOES TO CHILDREN

Of course such things are not without their effect on the children. In the promise which the Episcopal Church requires a prospective couple to sign before marriage, there appears among the purposes of marriage agreed to the phrase "the procreation of children." On the blank which one church had printed there was a typographical error and this appeared as "for the protection of children." This mistake was not too unhappy a one. In contemplating marriage a couple should take seriously what kind of matrix for the spiritual development of their children would be provided; and children, even unborn, are entitled to be protected against a divisive spiritual atmosphere or a family life running on two cylinders. A proper spiritual orientation for children is hard to come by in any case, because the best family is set in the midst of a very confused and dehydrating secular cultural pattern. In the midst of "every wind of doctrine" it is important that the family be a sort of "spiritual greenhouse" in which the right kind of religious responses can be cultivated in the children. A unity of conviction in the household enables a child to grow in grace on the basis of his respect and love for his parents. But assuming that the child does love and respect both of his parents he is bound to be confused when one regards as white what the other one takes for black, when one makes much of an institution which the other does not regard as worthy of allegiance. Even if a "peaceful" solution —silence about religious matters in the household—is achieved, this is all the more devastating; the possibility of the child's developing a sense of the relevance of religion to life as a whole becomes virtually nil.

Case 11. Fred, nine, does not get on well with the sister who teaches him in the parochial school; and furthermore he would rather go to the public school where most of his

little friends go. His father, who does not go to church at
all, can give him no convincing reasons why he should go
to the parochial school beyond "That is what your mother
and I have decided." In talking to his mother about it, Fred
says, "After all, Daddy went to a public school and it didn't
seem to hurt him any. And if he thinks it is so important
that I learn about the Catholic Church why doesn't he go
to church with us himself?"

Or the child's attitude may go even further.

Case 12. Winifred, ten, has always been more devoted
to her mother than to her father. Her father goes to Mass
every Sunday, but otherwise takes no particular interest in
Roman Catholic affairs and never talks about the matter at
home. Her mother, on the other hand, is one of the "pillars"
of the local Presbyterian Church, always comes home from
church enthusiastic about the service, the music and the
sermon and obviously enjoys herself at the other activities
during the week. She announces one day, "Mommy, I
would rather be what you are. It seems a whole lot better
to me." Assuming that the father might be able to communicate to his daughter convincing reasons for remaining a
Roman Catholic (though it is by no means sure that he
would have such "ammunition" at hand), what convincing
arguments could her *mother* give her? And what her mother
thinks really matters more to her in this case. How religiously nourishing is the answer, "Well, your father and I
agreed to that years ago and so we have to stick to it"?

Or the child's own religious lassitude or the distraction of
more worldly things can receive encouragement from the
mixed nature of the marriage.

Case 13. Tom, twelve, is tired of Sunday school and
would much rather take part in a baseball game which goes
on down the street at the same hour. His mother goes to

the eleven o'clock service, but his father stays home reading the paper and puttering around. "I don't want to go," says Tom. "Dad doesn't go and I don't see why I should. Dad is certainly as nice a man as some of those men down there who hang around the church all the time." Just what can Dad—or Mother—say that will be really convincing in the face of the living example of disinterest on the part of one of the two persons closest to the boy?

There is an increasing realization on the part of all the principal Churches that religious education cannot rest upon the slender reed of forty-five minutes a week of Sunday school instruction. The formation of the child's religious life and his convictions must, in large measure, take place in the home. There, he is being formed—for good or ill—by the atmosphere which surrounds him. The "Ligon Plan" used by many churches in a wide variety of denominations goes the farthest in its insistence upon parent involvement in the educative process. The United Presbyterian and the Episcopal curricula, developed in recent decades, also are going very far in this direction.

Obviously a home split on the subject of religion cannot serve to implement this type of sound religious education. For example, no one of the principal Churches teaches that ethics is the main thing and that it doesn't matter what a man believes. Yet, as is illustrated in some of the cases above, this view is actually what the child is deciding for because of the pattern in his home. He is either deciding this, or "downgrading" the deepest convictions and motivations of one of his parents—and neither of these procedures is to his good.

Grace at meals and family prayer and family Bible reading are being taken more seriously these days than they have been for many a decade. Yet if the head of the family is outside the fold the Roman Catholic wife and children may not even say "Amen" to the grace said by their father. They cannot participate in prayers led by other Christians, but must maintain a stony silence, and when it comes to the reading of the Bible, the King James Version or the Revised Standard Version can have no place; because they cannot hear it. Only a "Roman Catholic" translation is allowed to reach the eyes or ears of the Roman Catholic members of the family. If the other parent generously yields the point, then the conviction is reaffirmed that his religion and its rendering of the sacred books are something not authentic. Then, when it comes to a discussion of the meaning of the Scriptures read, he is forbidden by the antenuptial agreement to press the meanings that his religious background would impart to the texts, or to disagree one whit with the meanings which the footnotes to the Catholic translations rather explicitly point out.

Yes, "the protection of children" is an important end of marriage and their protection from spiritual injury is not easy in a mixed marriage. But to return to the correct word in the form to which we referred earlier—"procreation," our survey of the mixed marriage in operation will not be complete unless we consider the difficulties involved in this whole aspect of a mixed marriage.

❦

CHAPTER III

THE PROBLEM OF
BIRTH CONTROL

ONE OF THE chief tension points in "mixed marriages" between Roman Catholics and others centers around family decisions as to the limitation of childbirth. Those already involved in a mixed marriage need help on this point; those contemplating one need to know clearly in advance the exact shape of the problem that they will be facing if they carry through with their plans. (As has been indicated, should the couple decide to be married by a priest of the Roman Catholic Church, in many dioceses it is required that the non-Roman party sign a promise agreeing not to use contraceptive devices.)

Some people assume that there are no ethical issues involved in the matter of birth control, it being thought of as a medical or sociological question only; others entertain a sense of guilt (conscious or submerged) about the whole matter. For both groups it is important to draw out the implications for this particular field of conduct which derive from the general principles of religious ethics.

Incidentally, one of the chief tension points between Roman Catholics and others in the political arena is created by the desire of the Roman Catholic Church to maintain on the books legislation which supports its teaching. Effective po-

litical counteraction requires, among other things, the understanding of the respective ethical positions and implications.

First we will set forth, simply and fairly, the Roman Catholic teaching on the matter of birth control, before analyzing
the view which is consonant with the general ethical teaching
of non-Roman Christians. This latter analysis will apply also,
with some modification of concepts, to those of Jewish faith
(at least those not of Orthodox persuasion) and, in a measure,
to secularists who still decide ethical questions in terms of the
general framework of the Christian world view.

THE ROMAN CATHOLIC ATTITUDE TOWARD BIRTH CONTROL[1]

In Roman Catholic teaching there is no general positive duty
requiring couples to have children. (By "positive duty" we
mean one the violation of which constitutes a sin.) Instead
the problem is with certain particular modes of avoiding childbirth which are denominated as sinful. To illustrate the point,
if a couple who do not wish to have children should agree
(freely and without duress from either side) to abstain from
sexual intercourse in order to be sure of avoiding conception,
they are perfectly free to do so under Roman Catholic moral
law. This does not mean that the church would not *prefer*
for them to have children. In fact, since they are not required
to have them under this situation (and in one yet to be discussed in connection with the "rhythm" method), steps taken
to insure having children might be regarded as a "work of
supererogation," that is, a meritorious act over and above the
law. But *not* to have them would not be sinful.

The matter of sin enters in connection with the use of
certain *methods of birth control*. In short, there is an absolute
bar (under pain of mortal sin) against methods which the
church regards as "artificial" and a qualified bar against the
use of the "rhythm" method. The principal artificial methods

[1] See more fully: Noll, *A Catechism on Birth Control* (Our Sunday
Visitor Press, 1951); Lilly, *So You Believe in Birth Control* (Catholic
Information Society).

which are banned are: the use of contraceptive devices, coitus interruptus (that is, withdrawal before the occurrence of the male orgasm), direct sterilization, and abortion. All these are grouped together as unnatural interference with natural process, and as acts sinful in themselves entirely apart from the motivation.

According to Roman Catholic teaching, abortion is sinful under any and all circumstances—except one: namely, when the death of the foetus is a secondary result in connection with a necessary operation on the mother. Even when the physician knows that the death of the mother will result if the foetus continues in being or is born, it is regarded as wrong to take the life of the foetus in order to spare the mother. A direct abortion, even under these circumstances, is unqualifiedly denominated "murder"—a word which, incidentally, is somewhat carelessly applied by some Roman Catholic apologists to prevention of conception as well.

The "rhythm" method stands on a different footing than the "artificial" methods. This involves the deliberate selection of "safe" periods for intercourse and abstinence during other periods in the month. As to its propriety or sinfulness, the Roman Catholic Church provides no clean-cut answer. In fact, there is currently a debate going on among Roman Catholic moral theologians as to this whole matter.[2] All agree that there are some circumstances which justify the use of the method: for example, danger to the health of the mother through childbirth, or illness preventing one of the parents from helping in the rearing of the children (medical reasons); likelihood of mental abnormality or hereditary defect (eugenic reasons); lack of housing, overpopulation, likely absence of the husband, such as for military duty (social reasons); inability to provide decently for the children (economic reasons). If these reasons are not grave or do not exist at all, one school of thought would say that the practice of "rhythm" for a short

[2] See "Rhythm in Marriage" by Fr. Gerald Kelly, S.J., in *America*, May 3, 1952.

time would be a venial sin (that is, one which would not bar one from salvation) and a mortal sin if practiced for a long time, say five or six years. Others would say that once the family has had a "reasonable" number of children, that is, enough to insure that the couple has done its share in providing for the conservation of the race, they would no longer need such "justifying" reasons to practice "rhythm," but could do so without sin, provided there was mutual agreement between the parents and they could practice it "without spiritual harm." Some of the latter would add that having children beyond this conservational limit would still be pleasing to God, would be desirable as works good "above the law," "beyond the call of duty." Some would even commend Catholic couples who disregard the "justifying reasons" for the use of the "rhythm" method and, trusting to Divine Providence, continue to build a family. Though prudence would be exercised in recommending such a course, yet couples would be free to "take the risk" without sin in so doing.

In summary: (1) There is no positive duty (that is, under the pain of sin) to have children or to refrain from having children; (2) certain methods deemed "artificial" are in themselves wrong and may not be utilized without mortal sin; (3) the "rhythm" method is not sinful if certain justifying circumstances exist; (4) where the circumstances do not exist *and* there are four or five children in the family already, there is confusion as to whether the use of the "rhythm method" is a venial sin, a mortal sin, or not sinful at all.

RELIGIOUS AND ETHICAL FOUNDATIONS

Now we turn to an analysis of the ethics of birth control consonant with the theology of the reformed Churches. First, it is important that we have in mind certain basic ethical principles common to these Churches (whatever their other differences) which determine the difference in the respective attitudes toward birth control.

1. God not only created the world, He creates it. The initial

task of creating order out of chaos continues. Man is called to share this creative work with God—not as a mere channel (as in the case of material and animal processes) but as a free agent, left with a wide discretion as to the best and most effective ways of helping complete God's creation—each man within his own sphere of influence.

2. The freedom and the rationality which God has conferred upon man as a gift better to enable him to serve as a partner with Him in the development and management of the world, have given man the capacity to develop various tools and devices which can achieve a better relationship between means and ends.

3. All that man does either advances or retards God's purposes in the world; hence all that he does is *under judgment*. All of a man's resources, time and energy belong to God. All of a man's decisions about the use of these resources of time and energy are ethical decisions; that is, every human decision is one of *sin or no*. The Biblical law is *Thou shalt love thy God with all thy heart, mind, soul and strength.* Anything less is sin.

4. This means that there are no areas of human conduct which are morally neutral. Likewise there are no areas in which a man can do anything "extra" for God and thus gain extra merit. If what he does is a *good thing*, then not to do it would be a sin; doing it is not achieving anything above the law. God's law is a 100 per cent claim on us. *When ye have done all that ye have been commanded to do, say, We are unprofitable servants* (St. Lk. 17:10). A man must decide on each moral issue presented to him what course of action will have creative results rather than destructive ones. In many situations the decision involves not a clean-cut, black-and-white issue, but the weighing of possible destructive results against possible constructive ones. Often what is involved is a decision for the lesser of two evils. In making these decisions the individual cannot claim to be infallible, nor can he be expected to be. But he is responsible for purity of motivation,

careful analysis of the matters at stake, and the optimum adaptation of means to the end of achieving the will of God in the particular situation.

THE RESULTING ETHICS OF BIRTH CONTROL

Now we proceed to apply these foundation principles to the particular field under discussion.

Assume that a couple is trying to decide whether or not they should practice birth control. Except under unusual circumstances this is not a blanket decision for a lifetime; it must always be a decision as to the *here and now situation*. The first question—ahead of all other questions—is whether they ought to have a child. This is *a vocational choice* under God's judgment just as would be a young man's wrestling with the question of going into the ministry. It is a particular variant of the broad question, "What is the will of God for my life?" If the answer conscientiously reached by the couple is that they *should* have a child at this point in their married life, then they have a positive duty to do so, and any means used to prevent this fulfilling of the will of God would be sinful. This is true whether the method be abortion, contraception or abstinence from intercourse. More than that, if pregnancy did not result, they would have the positive duty of seeking medical advice, and taking any possible steps which might aid fertility.

On the other hand, if they conscientiously decide that they should not now be having a child, then they have a positive duty *not* to have one, and this duty, like all other ethical duties, requires the intelligent use of the most suitable means possible to achieve its fulfillment. It is important to note here that it is not said that under certain circumstances the use of the proper method of birth control is *licit* (that is, permissible for the couple); *it is their duty positive*. In Christian ethics no action is merely licit, since all of life is to be lived under God in positive fulfillment of what is conceived of as His will at each step along the way.

Once this basic decision is made, namely, whether or not the couple ought to have a child, the couple must next turn to a consideration of the most effective means, among the proper ones available, to carry out their decision. If the decision is to have a child, then normally intercourse without the use of contraceptive devices will in time achieve the result. If it does not, a physician can suggest the next steps. On the other hand, if the decision has been not to have a child, some method of birth control is indicated. The desirability of one mode over another should be decided on three bases: (1) the ethical character of the particular mode, in itself; (2) its effectiveness for birth prevention; and (3) the "side effects" of the use of the particular mode.

Now let us consider each of the methods of birth control in the light of these three tests.

1. *Abstinence.* This method rates well on the first two tests: it is not unethical in itself, and it obviously has maximum effectiveness for birth prevention. But it meets the third test (side effects) very poorly, since it robs the marriage of a basic element and is thus contrary to the will of God. Here we have to point out a basic cleavage in ethical teaching between the Roman Catholic Church and other traditions. The Roman Church teaches that the end of intercourse is procreation; other results are secondary. Others teach that intercourse has two primary functions: procreation is of course one; the other is that of a sacrament of union. Intercourse is "an outward and visible sign of an inward and spiritual grace" which is both effect and cause. It expresses the love and commitment that are already there and it also nourishes and inspires love and commitment. When the end of procreation is not a suitable end of marriage at the particular time, the other end still exists and should continue to be fulfilled. Any arrangement which would deny it is a wrong one and contrary to the will of God.

2. The *"rhythm method."* This method passes the first test (it is not wrong in itself), but it does not adequately pass the second and third. On the score of effectiveness the "rhythm

method" does not rate very high. If the period of ovulation were known for certain, the method would be effective by abstinence from intercourse for a period of approximately eight days per month. But since the period cannot be known for certain, varying even in the same individual and easily affected by various factors (such as fatigue, emotional stress, or illness), this method is quite "risky." As to the third test, the considerations which apply to abstinence have a limited application here: the marriage is denied its proper fulfillment, especially at times which may be those of greatest desire on the part of the wife.

3. *Coitus interruptus.* Withdrawal before orgasm is not wrong in itself, since within the marriage relationship affectionate expression is not limited to acts which culminate in orgasm every time, nor is there any particular mode or manner of sexual contact which is wrong in itself. But this method definitely does not pass the second and third tests. As to effectiveness, it presupposes more control than normally can be counted upon. And as to side effects, if this is to be the usual behavior it robs the couple of the closest embrace at the height of coitus and makes virtually impossible simultaneous orgasm, which is the optimum expression of the relationship.

4. *Contraceptive devices.* Now we come to the most usual method of birth control. Included in this category are the use of diaphragms, condoms, suppositories, douches, and pills, all designed, with varying degrees of effectiveness, to prevent the union of male spermatozoa and female ova. By definition the process is aimed at the *prevention* of life rather than (as in the case of abortion) the destruction of life which has already begun. This distinction is important when we apply the first test, namely, the inherent ethical quality of the act. There are only two bases on which the act could be regarded as inherently unethical: that it is a prevention of life, or that it is "artificial." To regard contraception as unethical because it is a *prevention* of life would prove too much: abstinence and the "rhythm method" also achieve this (and for that matter so

does clerical celibacy). To argue that it is artificial is also to prove too much: so are circumcision and appendectomy. To speak even more broadly, to rule out the use of devices which man's thought has developed for controlling natural processes would be to erase the meaning of the whole human enterprise from the Garden of Eden on; everything from dams for water power to the common haircut would be under the ban.

As to the second test (effectiveness) the most widely used of these methods are second only to complete abstinence. The relative effectiveness of each of the methods is a medical not an ethical matter; but the ethic is the motivation behind research toward, and the selection of, the most effective way.

These methods pass the third test (re "side effects") in varying degrees. The most recently developed means (the pill), when fully proven to have no physiological side effects, of course would provide no interference whatsoever with the sexual act as the fullest expression of union between spouses. As for the diaphragm, its use with some common sense about planning need not really interfere either. But these statements are subject to one qualification—if there are not guilt feelings about the matter. If there are such feelings, they need closer analysis: if they arise from a sense that there is a responsibility to have more children which is being thus avoided, then there *should be* a sense of guilt, because under these circumstances it is wrong to use contraception, "rhythm" or any other method. But if the conscience is clear on that score, there should be no guilt feelings, and one purpose of the analysis in this chapter is to allay them.

As a method, scientific contraceptive techniques pass all three tests most fully and in most circumstances represent the optimum solution.

5. *Abortion.* This method of birth prevention does not pass the first test: it is an act inherently wrong in itself. Since by definition it operates when life has come into being, to practice abortion is to kill; like all killing, it must normally be denominated as murder. However, there are some circum-

stances in which a killing is not murder; for example, killing in self-defense or in a war which one's conscience endorses. Even here, the killing is not a good thing, but it is the lesser of two evils. There are two such situations in the case of childbirth: (1) when the mother requires an operation (not directly connected with pregnancy) completion of which may involve taking the life of the child; and (2) where childbirth is likely to cause the death of the mother. Here a balance of interests is involved and it is not difficult to understand why most people would regard the life of the mother as more precious than that of the unborn child. The fact that her personality has matured, that she may have a wide web of responsibilities which are important and human relationships which are valuable, that she has an important place in the lives of others, all outweigh the quite unknown possibilities of a child who has not yet seen the light of day. Therefore, in this situation, it would be right to take every step to preserve the life of the mother; and it would be wrong to do otherwise. This is one illustration of the situation that often arises in the application of Christian ethics: factors are weighed on both sides of the matter and a decision made, not in terms of black-and-white, but in terms of the preponderance of the significant interests at stake. But things cannot so be laid out if in the balance against the quite serious matter of taking the life of the unborn child is merely the convenience of the parents or even matters affecting the health of the mother or the economic situation in the home. While these latter are significant factors in determining what is the will of God in terms of a contemplated childbirth if *prevention* of life is under consideration, they certainly do not outweigh the inherent evil of the *taking* of human life.

FACTORS INVOLVED IN THE DECISION AS TO CHILDBIRTH

Now that the various means of birth prevention have been analyzed in the light of general ethical principles, and the relation of means to ends has been seen, let us turn again to what is the No. 1 question for a couple to decide prayerfully under God: namely, should they, at this particular time, have a child? Obviously there are no pat answers to any such question, nor will even the most careful analysis of particular cases insure infallibility. Obviously too there can be no "standard" number of children to meet the requirements, such as the "four to five" suggested by some Roman Catholic writers. Yet certain considerations clearly should be taken into account. These are:

1. *Medical or eugenic factors*

Will the health of the mother be seriously impaired?

Are there factors—indicated by heredity and by the condition of the other children—to suggest that the health (physical or mental) of the child-to-be may be dubious?

Has due allowance been made for spacing between children?

2. *Economic or environmental factors*

Is there reasonable likelihood that there will be sufficient means to provide, in at least minimum decency, for the newborn child as it grows up? (This does not mean that the funds for the child's college education need already be in hand!)

Is the family adequately housed so that there will be sufficient living space for the newcomer?

3. *Psychological and other personal factors*

Is it likely that the parents will be able to provide sufficient personal attention to the growing child, in the light of the number of other children and other significant demands and commitments?

Are there threats to the continuity of normal home life, such as military service or perhaps the possibility of separation or divorce?

Are there deep-seated tensions in the home which are not yet resolved?

Now all of these aspects present fertile possibilities for rationalization of what is really selfishness; and thus there is more to be said, from the point of view of Christian ethics. First, unless the factor is obvious, a very careful searching of

conscience should precede any decision to practice contraception. And until a family has all the children that can be psychologically and economically managed, a decision not to have a
child would be the exception rather than the rule, a temporary
decision rather than a permanent one. And thus, *in case of
doubt, the decision would be to have children.* As an aid
against rationalizations and as a help toward an objective decision, if the question is a close one, it would be wise to take
counsel with one's minister and with one's physician.

It may seem to a Roman Catholic that such an approach to
the matter is "subjective" and indefinite. But the same approach
is necessary in many other fields of life (from the selection of
a spouse to the decision about one's vocation) and especially
under an ethical system where the whole of life is under the
moral law in terms of *sin or no,* and where the individual is
responsible under God for the use he makes of his life. It is
easier to be definite in a system which is a code of "don'ts"
dealing with standard situations. But even the Roman Catholic Church is not able to get away from the subjective element:
in the decision a couple must make about the "justifying
factors" for the use of the "rhythm method" almost precisely
the same variables as those analyzed above come into play.
(In fact the Roman Catholic literature dealing with this particular situation was of considerable help to the author in sug-
gesting the factors which should be weighed—not in connection with the use of any particular means but rather in deciding
the end—which is the primary question.)

IMPLICATIONS OF THE CONFLICT IN VIEWS

Now that we have sketched out an analysis of the ethics of
birth control according to the two principal approaches, a few
comments are appropriate as to the bearing of all this on mixed
marriages.

If what we have said as to the ethics of birth control added
up to a conviction that contraception, for example, is *permissible* in certain situations, it would appear that the conscience

of a Roman Catholic party to a mixed marriage (a conscience which suffers under a ban against contraception) ought to be respected, and one could appreciate why a Protestant, for example, would enter into an agreement to respect this conscientious scruple just as he might decide to go along with his spouse in the eating of fish rather than meat on Friday—since there is nothing in his religion which makes the eating of fish sinful. However, this is not the situation under the analysis which we have made. Obviously situations can arise in which the Roman Catholic party is forbidden to practice contraception in which the other party is under a duty *not* to have a child and under a duty to use the most effective methods possible for carrying out what he thus conceives to be the will of God. We have in such a situation not a contest between one under the law and one free to act either way as he wishes, but rather one between two people both of whom are under a moral stricture to act in opposite ways. The effect of such a tension upon two sincerely religious persons would be difficult to exaggerate. In fact it is difficult to see how anyone could in good conscience commit himself to such a situation in advance.

CHAPTER IV

"BUT WE'LL FIND A WAY
TO WORK IT OUT"

Bᴜᴛ ɴᴏ ᴀᴍᴏᴜɴᴛ of reasoning, no number of case histories necessarily downs the aphorism so typical of American culture: "Love will find a way!" So it is no surprise that the active minds of thousands of young people faced with the problem of mixed marriage have devised a number of formulae by which they can convince themselves that they will be able to bypass the obstacles in their path. Before taking up what are in fact the only two sound solutions, we will analyze the standard-brand pseudo-solutions.

1. "ᴡᴇ'ʟʟ ʟᴇᴛ ᴛʜᴇ ᴄʜɪʟᴅʀᴇɴ ᴄʜᴏᴏsᴇ ꜰᴏʀ ᴛʜᴇᴍsᴇʟᴠᴇs."

If by this the couple means that at the age of twenty-one or thereafter their offspring may decide their religious futures, then they have merely stated what is true in every case. Naturally any person, no longer under his parents' control, can become anything he wants to become. Increasingly these days adults do make their own religious choices—whatever they have been raised. But if by this statement the couple means that at some undefined age—say eight or twelve—the child will choose, one might ask what will be the basis of choice? How will a child of that age have a good grasp of all the significant alternatives? And is a child of that age competent to make what is so fundamental a choice and can he or she be relied upon to make the choice on the basis of the most significant issues rather than upon superficial considerations?

Furthermore, the children will in any case be growing up with a religio-ethical system. Everyone has a religion, that is, everyone has a set of premises taken on faith, which gives the meaning to his life and provides the basis of his judgments and the priority scale of values which are of significance to him. If God and the supernatural realities are to be left out of the child's spiritual diet, then he will feed upon humanistic, materialistic religious notions, whether or not the parents have decided for this result, or whether by making no decision, such notions have won by default. Responsiveness to the unseen realities is rather hard to come by in any case. While in the case of some people who have been denied training and nurture in this responsiveness, some great event in later life— some crisis, some crossroads—has opened them up to sensitiveness to God, on the whole it is more reliable to "install the wiring" for spiritual communication as early as possible in a young life. Whether the current will be on or off at given periods in the person's life later on is another question. But, the *capacity* for religious responsiveness is something which can be definitely cultivated and it is a direction in which children are especially malleable.

Now this particular approach may take the form of a more specific determination to instruct the child in ethics, in goodness to neighbor and in religious tolerance. This may be in fact what the parents want to have as the exclusive content of their child's religious experience through life—and it is their freedom so to decide—but let them not think that they have made no decision for the child. They have decided to raise him an Ethical Culturist. And Ethical Culture is a religion as much as Buddhism or Mormonism is. Now the fact that the parents do not intend to be making a religious choice for their child, perhaps even the fact that each of the parents in his own religion embraces more. supernatural content than does Ethical

Culture, only confuses the situation further for the child. He
is to be allowed to have some "lowest common denominator"
religion, yet observes that one or both of his parents are priz-
ing something that he's "not in on." A cloture on religious discussion has, we will assume, been agreed upon, and as a result
he is being denied the religious insights and experiences of
each of his parents.

> *Case 14.* David is Jewish, but generally goes to the syna-
> gogue only on high Holy Days. Katherine, his wife, goes to
> church about every other Sunday. By strict agreement his
> son, William, goes to church with neither of them, staying
> home with the non-attender while the other one goes. His
> curiosity, combined with the church-going experiences of
> his little friends, causes him to beg to go—sometimes with
> one, sometimes with the other. He is informed that he can
> go when he is older but that he isn't going now because his
> mother and father haven't had any disagreement over reli-
> gion yet, and they don't want to start now.

2. "WE'LL RAISE THEM BOTH WAYS AND LET THEM DECIDE."

If this solution could be worked out in full, the child would
probably have religious indigestion if not ecclesiastical schizo-
phrenia. But of course in practice he would not really be a
part of the life of either of the traditions. Denied the initiatory
rites of either of the traditions he cannot proceed to the second steps with his classmates (first Holy Communion, Confirmation, "joining the Church," bar mitzvah), he will not be
able to be regular in his attendance at Sunday school unless
by happy coincidence one of his parents is a Jew or a Seventh
Day Adventist. This solution presents a dilemma: if the two
religious traditions are close enough so that there will be no
serious conflict pattern set up in the child, then the solution is
not needed: the parents had better give careful study to the
denominations to which they adhere and choose between them
(more about this possibility is discussed in Chapter IX). On

the other hand, if there are significant differences between the two traditions there is also a dilemma: either (1) the child is related to them in a spectator or "balcony" sense—which is no way to "get religion" of any type or to nourish religious sincerity; or (2) he is entering as best he can into the spirit of the two traditions—in which case he is bound to be alerted sooner or later by the *yea-nays,* and as a child he is not in a position to work out an eclectic scheme of his own—if anyone can very successfully do that.

But some have sought to get around these difficulties by a still further solution:

3. "WE'LL RAISE THEM ONE THING AND THEN LET THEM CHOOSE LATER."

Whichever of the two is chosen represents an initial victory for one of the two parties—with all the difficulties this victory implies, as discussed above. If the child has no particular reason for being dissatisfied with the one chosen, nor has developed a point of reference from which to bring it under critical judgment, then he doubtless will choose the tradition in which he has been started, and the result is the same as if the one spouse had flatly yielded to the other, content to regard his own religion as of secondary importance. If, however, what the parents mean is that as an adult he can choose to be what he wants to be, that is not to say anything—because such is always the case.

Most prospective partners expect that they will have more than one child; this has suggested another solution that seems very fair, at first blush:

4. "WE WILL ALTERNATE THE CHILDREN RELIGIOUSLY."

This decision will have either of two results, neither of them desirable: It will mean to the children either that their parents regard the matter of religious conviction as unimportant or that it is important and hence there is a wall down the center of the family. Again, it means that the children will be inhibited from sharing their religious experience, or that their two religious allegiances will be placed on a competitive basis, with the parents as interested—but tactfully silent—bystanders. One thing we can be sure of: the children will not be particularly tactful in this regard.

Now we turn to another set of "ways out" which have particular reference to proposed marriages in which one of the parties is a Roman Catholic.

Sometimes the Roman Catholic party is not particularly loyal to the church, but is mainly concerned that the marriage be performed by a priest so that his parents will not be too upset. Often he has already agreed that the children will be raised otherwise or that one of the solutions quoted above will be resorted to—all of which, of course, is against the teaching of his Church and a violation of the promises which he and his spouse will be required to make. But they agree:

5. "WE WILL SIGN THE PROMISES, BUT WE WILL SECRETLY AGREE NOT TO KEEP THEM."

Obviously this is to start the marriage in a lie; but some couples rationalize around that by saying that it is a "white lie" to avoid hurting people who would not understand. But there are more complicated difficulties attendant upon this solution. First, even by signing the promises (regardless of the intent to keep them, the non-Roman party makes a very poor witness with the Roman Catholic party's family, because he or she goes on record as saying that his religious allegiance is not of enough importance to him to safeguard it for his children. Further, the problem is not over when the priest has pronounced them man and wife.

Case 15. Francis, a nominal Roman Catholic, and Ethel, an active Baptist, sign the antenuptial agreement required by the Roman Catholic Church, but secretly agree that the children will be raised in Ethel's faith. Their first child is now a year old and has not been baptized because Ethel's Church does not believe in infant baptism. However, every time that they see Francis' parents, the latter ask when the child is going to be baptized, assuming of course that the baby will be baptized by a priest. The situation grows increasingly embarrassing.

In the illustration "the hurt" to the parents which the original scheme was seeking to avoid is now going to strike them with full force—or else Ethel is going to find herself yielding to the pressures of her mother-in-law and father-in-law, with the postponement of the application of the secret agreement until the time that the child is to begin Sunday school. Then the same problem will come up again in full force.

Sometimes a nominal Roman Catholic is indifferent enough about his religion to enter into a secret agreement annulling the antenuptial contract, but after his first child he begins to be nostalgic about his religious heritage and wishes that the child could be christened and ultimately sent to a Roman Catholic school. By this time he may even have returned to the sacraments himself and realizes that unless the antenuptial agreement is carried through he will not be able to make a good confession and receive communion. If he decides to be a "gentleman" and not raise the issue again he has inner difficulties of conscience which he can ill suppress. If, on the other hand, he does raise it, a basic cleavage in the marriage is created and his wife cannot help but feel that he "hoodwinked" her into making the agreement—and she will be less inclined than ever to keep it as written.

Much the same difficulty occurs when the couple has decided to bypass the difficulty involved in the Roman Catholic attitude on birth control. This is a problem which is broader than the matter of mixed marriages, but is particularly acute there. Many a Roman Catholic has decided to follow his own mind on the subject, simply making a personal exception to the teaching of the church. Statistics of birth control clinics give ground to believe that this is a very widespread attitude. Now on the face of it it may seem plausible enough to the non-Roman party when the couple agrees:

6. "WE'LL GO AHEAD AND USE CONTRACEPTION, REGARDLESS OF WHAT ANY CHURCH SAYS."

The other party is likely to accept this arrangement because in his own religious heritage personal exceptions to the official teaching of the Church may be fairly commonplace and need not seriously disturb his membership in, or sympathy for, a particular tradition. Let us say that the prospective groom is a Methodist and his church teaches that drinking is wrong. Nevertheless he drinks moderately and it does not particularly bother his conscience. So when his prospective bride tells him that she will treat birth control much the same way it seems plausible enough to him. But he is overlooking two factors in the religious life of a Roman Catholic which do not necessarily exist in the religious life of a Protestant.

First of all, there is an "all or nothing" character to Roman Catholicism because of its theory about authority. The government of the church is entrusted to the Pope, who is viewed as infallible when speaking officially on matters of faith or morals. Now, in the nature of the case, infallibility depends upon not "missing" even once. A thoughtful Roman Catholic who, on rational grounds, has made an exception acceptable to him on the matter of birth control cannot help but see that he is no longer viewing the Pope as infallible. In this conclusion he is denying a cardinal tenet of the Church, on which many other tenets depend. The denial then creates a serious strain on his faith which may result in his either losing it entirely or giving up his special views on birth control. Pressure toward the latter solution comes because of a second factor, not usually operative in the case of the other party.

This second factor is the confessional. If a Roman Catholic conceals a sin in confession, then the entire confession is invalid and the absolution ineffective. The decision of many a woman to ignore the sin of contraception in making her confession puts her in a condition of very uneasy conscience because of her quite understandable doubt about the validity of her own position, for there hangs upon the validity of her position the validity of her whole confession and her right to receive Holy Communion. Roman Catholics are taught—reasonably enough—that it is a grievous sin to receive Holy Communion when one is not in a state of grace; thus sin is added to sin in her contemplation of her condition and this feeling of sinfulness is hardly the most suitable psychological attitude to have associated with her most intimate relationship with her husband. Whether consciously dwelt upon or suppressed, it is not a healthy state of mind. However, if she goes ahead and tells the priest that she is using contraception at least she has suppressed nothing; but absolution will not be given to her, even for the sins which she has confessed and repented—unless she can affirm a sense of repentance about the use of contraception. And true repentance includes a "firm purpose of amendment." To repent each time, intending not to do it again, and then to return to the practice, is to court a cynicism about the whole ethical and sacramental life which will ultimately be devastating to the personality and deteriorating as to her relations to her husband.

This crisis is somewhat pointed up by the fact that these days priests quite customarily inquire in the confessional as to whether the penitent is married and, if so, whether she uses contraception. Very few persons—Roman Catholics or otherwise—have minds sufficiently compartmentalized that they can brazenly say no when the answer is yes and yet believe in the validity of the rest of the experience.

Now that we have given realistic attention to the mixed marriage in operation and have shown the inadequacy of the usual "solutions" people offer, perhaps we are in a position to be reasonably sympathetic to the dim view which the various Churches take toward mixed marriages.

CHAPTER V

※

THE ROMAN CATHOLIC RULES

THE FIRST THING to understand about the Roman Catholic position is this: *a mixed marriage is not a good thing.* This point is missed by many people because the Roman Catholic Church has such well-organized machinery for arranging mixed marriages. People tend to assume that *if* the conditions required by the Church are met the Church is quite happy with the outcome. Actually this is not the case. The Roman Church recognizes, as does any other religious group, that the deepest spiritual union is lacking when there is not a common basis of faith. This point seems to have been missed by many of the Roman Catholic laity, if we can judge from a poll already referred to, in which only about half of the Roman Catholics registered any objection to mixed marriages (see page 27).

THE BASIC ROMAN CATHOLIC ATTITUDE

We should ponder the words of Pope Pius XI in his encyclical *Casti connubii* (§§ 82 and 85):

This attitude of the church to mixed marriages appears in many of her documents, all of which are summed up in the Code of Canon Law: "Everywhere and with the greatest strictness the Church forbids marriages between baptized persons, one of whom is a Catholic and the other a member of a schismatical or heretical sect; and if there is added to this the danger of the falling away of the Catholic party and the perversion of the children, such a marriage is forbidden also by the divine law." If the Church occasionally on account of circumstances does not refuse to grant a dispensation from these strict laws (provided that the divine law remains intact and the dangers above mentioned are provided against by suitable safeguards), it is unlikely that the Catholic party will not suffer some detriment from such a marriage. . . .

Assuredly, also, there will be wanting that close union of spirit which as it is the sign and mark of the Church of Christ, so also should be the sign of Christian wedlock, its glory and adornment. For, where there exists diversity of mind, truth and feeling, the bond of union of mind and heart is wont to be broken, or at least weakened. From this comes the danger lest the love of man and wife grow cold, and the peace and happiness of family life, resting as it does on union of hearts, be destroyed.

The reason why not even Roman Catholics have sufficiently understood this position is that, contrary to the encyclical just quoted ("If the Church occasionally on account of circumstances does not refuse to grant dispensation from these strict laws . . ."), the Church rather regularly grants a dispensation upon the signing of the antenuptial agreement, forwarded to the bishop. Furthermore people tend to assume that more often than not the Roman Catholic Church is the gainer from mixed marriages, since the children, under an antenuptial agreement, are to be brought up Roman Catholics and since it often is assumed that the other partner will probably end up becoming a Roman Catholic. Actually this is not the case. In many mixed marriages the non-Roman party declines to sign the antenuptial agreement and the Roman party is married in such a way (outside of the Church) that he becomes excommunicated. Even when the antenuptial agreement is signed it is often not kept.[1] And, even where it is kept, the children often in fact fall away, either following the example of their

[1] See the Brooklyn [Roman Catholic] *Tablet,* April 3, 1954, p. 14.

non-Roman parent in religion or losing their interest in religion entirely because of the conflict pattern which religion seems to set up in the family with which they are most familiar. Or the Roman Catholic party, out of touch with the influence of parents and other Roman Catholic associations, often tends to drift away from the Church, especially if he or she is under the pressure of moral conflict in such realms as that of birth control.

When none of these results follow, the fact is that a mixed marriage can in no wise meet the test of a truly Christian marriage as conceived by the Roman Catholic Church: that of a couple united in the mystical body of Christ, expressing this union in a common participation in the sacraments and by a common concern for the success of the Church on earth and in heaven. The Church's lack of enthusiasm for the marriage is shown by the fact that until recently even when all the formalities for dispensation had been gone through, the marriage itself could not be conducted in church. Now in a good many dioceses this rule has been changed; but until recent years in all places a mixed marriage was a drab affair conducted in the rectory parlor with the priest vested only in his black cassock and with the service conducted in a way slightly less perfunctory than a justice of the peace ceremony. The omission of the blessing is significant as to the attitude of the Church toward such a marriage. Now that under the rules of some dioceses the wedding may be conducted in a church the service is still not the regular marriage ceremony of the Church. It is not conducted at the altar. The blessing and other beautiful elements are missing. All of this points to the fact that this is not the Church's idea of a good marriage.

HOW SUCH MARRIAGES ARE ARRANGED

Yet such marriages do occur in considerable numbers with the approval of the Church. How is this arranged? The authority which makes the rules may dispense with the rules. The canon law of the Church provides that on application through the pastor of the church a mixed marriage may be permitted by the bishop, who has the authority to issue a "dispensation." This is granted as a matter of course if the antenuptial agreement is signed.

The exact form of the antenuptial agreement varies from diocese to diocese, but almost universally these days it consists of four elements, and increasingly throughout the dioceses, of a fifth. The four "standard" elements are these:

1. A promise of the non-Roman party that he will in no way seek to obstruct, hinder or persuade the Roman Catholic in the practice of his religion.

2. A promise by the Roman Catholic party to seek by every means at his disposal to convert the non-Roman party to his religion.

3. A promise of both parties that the children of the marriage will be baptized and educated in the Roman Catholic faith.

4. A promise that a civil or Protestant ceremony will not be conducted.

The fifth promise, not universal, is that contraceptive devices will not be used contrary to the teachings of the Roman Catholic Church.

The wording of a typical antenuptial agreement (without the fifth promise) is as follows:

I, the undersigned, not a member of the Catholic Church, wishing to contract marriage with ...., a member of the Catholic Church, propose to do so with the understanding that the marriage bond thus contracted is indissoluble, except by death. I promise on my word and honor that I will not in any way hinder or obstruct the said ...., in the exercise of ... religion and that all children of either sex born of our marriage shall be baptized and educated in the Catholic faith and according to the teaching of the Catholic Church, even though the said .... should be taken away by death. I further promise that I will marry ... only according to the marriage rite of the Catholic Church, that I will not either

before or after the Catholic ceremony, present myself with ...
for marriage before a civil magistrate or minister of the gospel.
Signature.....................
Signed in the presence of Rev. ....
Place .... Date ....

On the reverse of this promise is one requiring the Roman
Catholic party to promise to do all in his power by word and
example, to bring about the conversion of the non-Roman
party.

Another safeguard to the integrity of the Roman party's religious faith is the insistence that the other party take instruction in the Roman Catholic faith. The reason given for this is
a sound one in itself: namely, that the non-Roman spouse may
better understand what his Roman partner is about in his religious life and thus may more sympathetically adjust to it. But
there is back of this the quite legitimate hope that in the
course of a series of instructions in the Roman Catholic faith
the non-Roman party may be attracted to consider coming into
the church.

To return to the promises in the antenuptial agreement, to
each a few words of commentary are in order:

1. The first promise means that the normal enthusiasms of
a spouse, by the expression of which his own convictions become attractive, are hampered. Obviously these days the non-
Roman party is not actually going to prevent the Roman Catholic from attending church or receiving the sacraments, in
sickness or in health. The real point is that argument or discussion tending toward establishing a "case" for the non-Roman
party's religion is ruled out.

2. Here is the reverse side of the coin. Whereas the non-
Roman party is to keep his mouth closed, the Roman party is
obligated to try in every way to attract and convince the non-
Roman party.

3. This is not simply a negative proviso by which the non-
Roman party relinquishes his control over the religious nurture

of the children; he is put under a positive obligation to provide a Roman Catholic education for his children, entirely apart from the activity—even the earthly existence—of the Roman party.

4. The prohibition of dual ceremonies rules out another of the "ways out" couples naïvely conceive, and is another illustration of the "Jim-Crow" attitude toward the non-Roman party's Church.

5. Here the non-Roman party agrees to operate, as to the procreation of children, under an ethical system which may in some particular situation correspond with that of his own, but which in other cases, as we have seen above, involves a direct conflict with his own ethical outlook.

THE ENFORCEMENT OF THE PROMISES

How can the Church enforce these promises? The Church has no legal remedy; nor has the Roman Catholic party so long as the marriage is intact. No court would take upon itself the regulation of matters which are so connected with the inner life of the family.[2] What about the enforcement of the antenuptial agreement after the breakup of a marriage? Will it be determinative as to which spouse receives custody of the children? Or if the non-Roman party is given custody will he or she be compelled by the decree to maintain the Roman Catholic upbringing of the children? Almost uniformly the court decisions have made clear that an antenuptial agreement has no such effect.[3]

[2] See People ex. rel. Sisson 271 N. Y. 285 (1936).
[3] See, for example, McLaughlin v. McLaughlin, 20 Conn. Supp. 278, 132 A.2d 420 (1957); Stanton v. Stanton, 213 Ga. 545, 100 S.E.2d 289; Lynch v. Uhlenhopp, 248 Iowa 68, 78 N.W.2d 491 (1956); Dumais v. Dumais, 152 Me. 24, 122 A.2d 322 (1956); Hackett v. Hackett, 78 Ohio L. Abs. 485, 150 N.E. 2d 431 (1957), app. dism'd, 168 Ohio St. 373, 154 N.E.2d 820; in re Butcher's Estate, 266 Pa. 479, 109 Atl. 683 (1920); Denton v. James, 107 Kan. 729, 193 Pac. 307 (1920); In re Dixon, 254 Mo. 663, 163 S.W. 827 (1914); State ex rel. Baker v. Bird, 253 Mo. 529, 162 S.W. 119 (1913); Brewer v. Cary, 148 Mo. App. 193, 127 S.W. 685 (1910); Boerger v. Boerger, 26 N.J. Super. 90, 97A.2d 419 (1943); In re Walsh's Estate, 100 Cal. App. 2d 194, 233 P.2d 578 (1950); In re Guardianship of Walsh, 114 Cal. App. 2d 82, 249 P.2d 578 (1953).

It is well established that in determining custody the prevailing factor is not supposed "rights" of a spouse, but the total welfare of the child.[4] And the courts are loath to interfere with the decisions as to religious upbringing made by the party who in fact has custody—usually the mother. In a somewhat unusual decision a lower New York court did flatly enforce an antenuptial agreement,[5] but later the New York Supreme Court in citing this case modified the position by saying that it was "charged with a responsibility even more impelling than the rights of this [Roman Catholic] father. The controlling consideration here is the welfare of the children"—which in this situation the court felt would be best served by continuing the Roman Catholic upbringing.[6] In a New Jersey decision, the court said:

To invoke the principle of estoppel against the plaintiff because of her ante-nuptial agreement, as defendant urges, would be to disregard the overriding consideration of what is best for the children and to determine—arbitrarily—their future welfare by an act with which they had nothing to do. In addition, it would deprive the mother of her right to change her mind—to choose a religion which apparently gives her greater spiritual comfort—and to inculcate in the children entrusted to her custody the religious principles which, for the time being, seem to her best. For like reasons, the court will not adopt defendant's contention that there has been an abandonment or waiver by plaintiff of her right, as custodian, to give other than Catholic training to her daughters.[7]

And, of interest as to the ethical principles at stake (later to be discussed) is the court's reliance upon the reasoning summarized in an article in the *Harvard Law Review*—based on prior court decisions. The author said:

[4] 49 Harv. L. Rev. 931 (1936); 36 Col. L. Rev. 678 (1936); 39 Am. Jur., Parent & Child, § 50, p. 684.

[5] Roman v. Roman, 34 N.Y.S.2d 100 (N.Y.C. Dom. Rel. Ct. 1942).

[6] Shearer v. Shearer, 73 N.Y.S. 2d 337, 358 (Sup. Ct., Steuben Co.). 1947.

[7] Boerger v. Boerger, 26 N.J. Super. 90, 97 A.2d 419 (1943).

No mere agreement as to the religious education of children between father and mother before or after marriage is binding and it is always open to either parent to change his mind, as it is his privilege to inculcate upon his children those religious principles which for the time being seem to him best. Some decisions base this fundamental principle on a public policy that a parent in the interest of morality should not be held to bind himself conclusively to relinquish control over his children's religious education. Especially must this appeal to those who regard this right as vested in the parents solely for the benefit of their children. Other authorities, however, rest these decisions rather on the practical conditions arising out of ordinary family life. . . .

It is further pointed out that for a breach of a contract of a parent concerning the religious education of a child no damages can be recovered and it cannot be enforced by a suit for specific performance.[8]

A number of courts have nullified antenuptial agreements on a ground no less fundamental than the First Amendment to the Constitution (and/or its State counterpart). In one such case the court concluded that such an agreement "was merely persuasive upon" the marrying father. The court concluded flatly:

. . . the courts have no authority over that part of a child's training which consists in religious discipline, and in a dispute relating to custody, religious views afford no ground for depriving a parent of custody who is otherwise qualified.[9]

Though the courts in New York State have not gone so far as to rest the matter on Constitutional grounds, the two most important decisions certainly give no basis for positive recognition of antenuptial agreements. In one case a lower court had

[8] Friedman, *The Parental Right to Control the Religious Education of a Child*, 29 Harv. L. Rev. 485, 492 (1916). See the more recent treatment by Leo Pfeffer, *Religion in the Upbringing of Children* 35 Bost. U. L. Rev. 333 (1955), which has been very helpful in the revision of this part of the book. See also Note, Enforceability of Ante-nuptial Contracts in Mixed Marriages, 50 Yale L.J. 1286 (1941).

[9] Denton v. James, 107 Kan. 729, 193 Pac. 307 (1920).

included in its separation decree a directive that the Christian Science mother raise the child a Roman Catholic; then later the mother asked for a modification to allow her boy to attend public school and receive instruction in Christian Science. Her request was granted and the action of the lower court was affirmed by both the intermediate appellate court and by the highest court in the State.

In a recent New York case, the lower court had awarded custody to the father because the mother declared plainly that she would *not* carry out the antenuptial agreement. This decision was reversed by the higher court on the ground that "what is best for the children" is paramount and the court felt that "the welfare of such very young children will be better served by allowing them to remain with their mother." [10]

It is evident then that the antenuptial agreement has little or no standing in the law.

However, as to enforcement of its position during the duration of the marriage the Roman Catholic Church has certain ecclesiastical sanctions.

First, let us consider the sanction enforcing the requirement of the signing of an antenuptial agreement. If the marriage is performed by a non-Roman minister or justice of the peace the Roman Catholic Church does not recognize the marriage at all; as a result, the parties are viewed as living in a state of sin. In addition to the first sin of participating in a "non-Catholic" rite, which under canon law brings the penalty of excommunication, each act of intercourse between the partners is viewed as a single occasion, and each such act is an additional mortal sin. Such sins as these could be forgiven in any case only through repentance—including firm purpose of amendment (a difficult psychological feat if the couple is really in love); but here there is the additional difficulty that the privilege of con-

---

[10] Begley v. Begley, 211 N.Y.S. 2d; 1004 (App. Div., 1961). The court dodged the question of the enforceability of the agreement, saying "that question may be presented at a later time when the children shall have reached an age which makes them less dependent on mother-care and which gives them sufficient maturity to receive religious instruction."

fession and absolution is not available since because of the sin of "attempted marriage" the party is cut off from all the sacraments of the church (unless in imminent danger of death). The only way this can be remedied is for the non-Roman party now to agree to make the promises and to be married before a priest.[11] Until then the Roman party is cut off from his church and from his accustomed religious life.

So seriously does the Roman Catholic Church take the invalidity of the marriage that should the couple separate and the Roman Catholic party receive a civil dissolution of marriage he would be entirely free—as far as the Roman Catholic Church is concerned—to contract another marriage, in spite of the church's usual rule against remarriage after divorce.

If there was an explicit private promise that the antenuptial agreement would not be lived up to, or if it could be shown that the non-Roman party entered into the antenuptial agreement in bad faith, not intending to keep it, then the marriage —even though before the Roman priest—can be declared invalid by annulment proceedings before the ecclesiastical court, thus permitting the Roman Catholic party to contract another marriage (on the assumption, of course, that a civil dissolution has taken place).

If the promises were in fact made in good faith, the later failure to observe them would place the Roman Catholic party in a state of sin, forgivable only upon intention now to keep the promises.

As to the strictures against contraception, the same sanctions are present as for any other act which the Roman Catholic Church deems a sin. Each separate use of a contraceptive device constitutes a mortal sin. Like any other sin it may be confessed and absolution given. But as we have indicated above, one of the conditions of absolution is, quite reasonably,

[11] An attempt of a Roman Catholic wife to force this solution by denial of sexual intercourse gave rise to the case of Diemer v. Diemer, 8 N.Y.2d 206 (1960), in which the court of appeals adjudged her religious scruples an insufficient justification for her denial and granted the husband a separation on the ground of "abandonment."

true repentance—and this obviously includes intention not to sin again. Repeated—say, weekly—confession of this same offense will lead the confessor (that is, the priest)—and for that matter the penitent—to the conclusion that there was not real repentance; and hence that absolution should not be received. Should the party decide to omit or conceal the matter, then according to Roman Catholic teaching his entire confession is invalid and his receiving of Holy Communion is a sacrilege— which is simply to add sin to sin. And as it is pointed out above, it is increasingly difficult these days under modern confessional practice, for female penitents at least, to conceal the use of contraception—except by direct lie in the confessional.

The Roman Catholic canon law is so set up that, when understood, it should be sufficient to discourage even the most hardy and individualistic souls from an optimistic "we'll work things out somehow" approach.

CHAPTER VI

THE ETHIC OF THE OTHER CHURCHES

THE TITLE OF this chapter is different from the last because the other churches are, by and large, not equipped with a neat set of rules on subjects like mixed marriages. Is this a sign of inefficiency, of moral flabbiness, lack of courage, or lack of seriousness about such matters? Perhaps any or all of these factors may play some part in one or another of the Churches, but basically there is another reason for the lack of specific regulations. The existence of a rule or regulation issued by the Church is not as crucial to other Christians as it is to a Roman Catholic. That is because of this important difference in the traditions: for the Roman Catholic something is wrong or right because the Church says so; for other Christians a thing *is* wrong or right, and they hope their Church knows which is which. In other words, for them a thing is not *made* wrong or right because the Church has spoken. This does not mean that it is not the Church's task to point out the issues at stake, to affirm the basic ethical principles involved and even draw conclusions from these principles which directly relate to the conduct in question. In fact all the principal non-Roman groups have done this very thing in the case of mixed marriages. The fact that they have done so only recently is perhaps not to their credit; yet we must remember that they were slow to feel the pressure of the rising rate of mixed marriages (for reasons pointed out in the first chapter). But in any case the principles at stake were there before the Churches declared them. Therefore, our procedure here will be to analyze these principles, beginning with the most fundamental claims of Christian ethics and then set forth the resolutions adopted by the governing agencies of several of the principal bodies.

A POSITIVE RESPONSIBILITY IS INVOLVED

To be true to its character, the ethic of the reformed Churches would have to start with the assertion of the positive responsibilities of the individual. The most basic responsibility involved in the case of the religious nurture of the children is this: a parent is under obligation to bring into the life of his child the maximum possibilities of religious fulfillment. This means that he is under responsibility to bring up his child in that religious heritage which he (the parent) sincerely believes is nearest to the full truth; narrowing the problem down to a choice between Christian traditions, the parent is under obligation to bring into the life of the child that view of Christianity which has the best understanding of God, of man, of man's salvation through Jesus Christ, and best provides the means of grace therefor. Granting that men do—and may reasonably—differ as to which is the truest and best way, yet when a parent honestly believes that one way is better than another, he must provide for his children that which he himself believes is the best. He can in good conscience do no less. As a Roman Catholic author has put it: "If [a devout Lutheran] is convinced that Lutheranism is right and Catholicism wrong, how can he conscientiously sign an agreement permitting his children to be reared in what he considers a false and erroneous creed?" [1]

This responsibility for the best spiritual nurture he can give

[1] Ginder, *A Mixed Marriage* (Catholic Information Society), p. 12.

his children is analogous to his responsibility for the best physical nurture and the best mental nurture. Some may think that baby food X is better than baby food Y, but if the parent really believes that baby food Y will be the best for his child he is under a moral obligation to use baby food Y, particularly if he is conscious of certain defects in baby food X which he believes do not exist in baby food Y.

These decisions that the parent must make will of course not bind the child forever. When he is out of school a young man may decide to read nothing thereafter but detective stories and horror comics, but while he is in school the parent quite reasonably backs up efforts to have him read Hawthorne, Tennyson and Shakespeare. A parent insists upon his child eating vegetables, fully aware of the fact that when he is grown up he will be perfectly free to eat nothing but meat and potatoes all his life. Parents make decisions for their children as to their mental and physical intake; they cannot avoid making the decision as to the spiritual intake—and they must make it on exactly the same basis: what they conscientiously think is best. To give a child less than what the parent thinks is the best (if the best is available) is a moral fault in the parent—whether we are talking about religion, feeding or education.

THE RESPONSIBILITY IS NOT DELEGABLE

Second, this responsibility for the spiritual nurture of children is something which may not be delegated or transferred to others. A parent has the right and duty to participate actively in the communication of spiritual truth and meaning to his child; he is not free to "drop out" of that phase of the child's life. If someone acts for him in this regard for a period (at a boarding school, for example), he has the responsibility of seeing that he chooses a delegate for this purpose whom he can trust to carry out this responsibility on the best level, that is, the level he believes is best. In no case can he make any final delegation, which is not revocable, to any other agency. His responsibility continues at all times.

Third, any attempt at such transfer of responsibility is ethically void. A man may by contract give up his *rights,* but he may not by contract give up his *responsibilities*. If parents entered into a contract with a nutrition laboratory whereby they agreed to feed their child substandard food for two years in order that the laboratory might observe the effect upon the child, such a contract would be ethically void *ab initio*. No matter what one writes down or signs, one's responsibilities remain. The realm under consideration is no exception. Even if a parent has agreed that his child should be brought up in another religious tradition, if the parent genuinely believes that his spiritual tradition is a better and more wholesome one, he is still under the responsibility to seek to communicate that which he conceives to be the best heritage. A man cannot in good conscience say to God, "I don't have to do my duty in this regard because I promised that I wouldn't."

THE INEVITABLE DILEMMA

An attempt so to contract away one's responsibilities is a sin, for it represents a decision not to carry out the will of God, in order to achieve some lesser aim. Like all sins it may be repented of, but repentance—under any system of ethics—requires "a firm purpose of amendment." In this case true repentance includes an intention to remedy the situation, to begin to do the duty which one had forsworn. But if the religious education of the child has already been started along another line usually it is not easy to rewrite the past and start over again. The other party has acted in reliance on the promises. Furthermore, both parties have a positive obligation to try to maintain the family unity. Insistence upon instructing the child in another faith might at this point seriously imperil the marriage. Thus the "signing" party is put in a moral dilemma: either answer is, in a measure at least, the wrong answer. How he may resolve this dilemma is discussed in a later chapter. It will suffice now to say that it is clear that a person cannot in good conscience get himself into a situation in which such a dilemma will arise. He cannot in good conscience contract a marriage under conditions which require him to promise not to fulfill one of his primary responsibilities as a parent, a responsibility which he cannot conscientiously give over to others: namely, the spiritual nurture of his children.

This is the thinking behind the official statements which have been made by the principal non-Roman religious bodies. Now let us examine the texts of these statements (which are arranged alphabetically).

ANGLICAN COMMUNION (including EPISCOPAL CHURCH)

The Church's Discipline in Marriage (Resolution)

The conference earnestly warns members of our Communion against contracting marriages with Roman Catholics under the conditions imposed by modern Roman Canon Law, especially as these conditions involve, among other things, a promise to have their children brought up in a religious system which they cannot themselves accept.

The Church's Discipline in Marriage (Committee Report)

A mixed marriage may be (1) a marriage between a Christian and a non-Christian; (2) a marriage between members of different Christian communions.

1. Marriage of a Christian with a non-Christian is a special concern in missionary provinces and dioceses, and local conditions and problems vary. In India the situation is complicated by certain legal requirements, but there is no doubt that the practice is increasing and extending among Indian Christians of high caste origin, a practice which may involve a technical abjuration of the Christian Faith: in Africa the practice of polygamy requires special consideration, but this was largely dealt with by the Lambeth Conference of 1920. (Resolution 39 and the section Holy Matrimony in the Report of the Committee on Missionary Problems.)

Each province must be left to work out the details of its discipline, but this Committee agrees that *these mixed marriages should be forbidden, except in cases approved by the bishop* of the diocese who has the power of granting dispensation.

2. In regard to marriage between an Anglican and a member of another Communion, it is important to remember that the *religious education and spiritual training of their children by word and example is a paramount duty of parents and should never be neglected nor left entirely to others.* It sometimes happens that, as a condition of marriage, one of the partners is required to sign a declaration that children born of the marriage will be brought up in the practice of a religious system in which he or she does not believe. *To give such an undertaking is a sin* as it is an abrogation of a primary duty of parents to their children. Young Church people must be taught to seek their future partners among those with whom they may be at one in this vital respect. Otherwise they imperil their own and each other's religious life, make complete union impossible, and put a great stumbling-block in the way of their children. *We strongly deprecate such mixed marriages,* and we assert that *in no circumstances* should an Anglican give any undertaking, as a condition of marriage, that the children should be brought up in the practice of another Communion.[2]

Resolved, that this Convention earnestly warns members of our Church against contracting marriages with Roman Catholics under the conditions imposed by modern Roman Canon Law, especially as these conditions involve a promise to have their children brought up in a religious system which they cannot themselves accept; and, further, because the religious education and spiritual training of their children by word and example is a paramount duty of parents and should never be neglected nor left entirely to others, we assert that in no circumstance should a member of this Church give any understanding, as a condition of marriage, that the children should be brought up in the practice of another Communion.[3]

BAPTIST, AMERICAN

The 1956 Convention of the American Baptist Churches noted critically "a growing tendency for young people to take a tolerant and permissive attitude towards inter-faith marriage."

Whereas, the Roman Catholic Church has published a direc-

[2] Lambeth Conference (1948), Resolution and Committee Report V(A).
[3] Resolution of General Convention of the Protestant Episcopal Church, San Francisco, California, 1949.

tive to its priests, church members and the general public imply-
ing that non-Catholic marriages lack the authenticity furnished by
Roman Catholic ceremonies through instituting disparaging re-
strictions and exceptions; and

Whereas, the publication of these discriminations affects so
many young people who unite in marriage in the freedom of our
American customs and indicates to them that non-Catholic marriages are of an inferior and less religious nature; therefore be it

Resolved, that the Northern Baptist Convention repudiate the
Roman Catholic claim to authoritarianism in marriage and declare
it an invasion of the principles of religious and social freedom.
Furthermore, be it

Resolved, that Baptist pastors be urged to inform their young
people of the menace to their freedom of the imposed authoritarianism of the Roman Catholic Church, not merely in the performance of marriage but also in the dictated rules regarding the
raising of offspring of mixed marriages in the Roman Catholic
Church; and that young people contemplating an interfaith marriage be instructed by their pastors regarding their civil and religious rights under our Baptist standards of religious liberty.[4]

Baptist, Southern

Whereas the Roman Catholic hierarchy has adopted a policy
to discourage mixed marriage and said church has sought to exact
from non-Catholic parties to mixed marriage pledges that said
marriages will be performed only by Catholic priests and that
children born to that union shall be brought up in the Catholic
faith; Therefore, be it

Resolved, first, that we, with our Roman friends, give public
warning of the dangers to harmonious home life in mixed marriages;

Second, that our churches under the leadership of their pastors
undertake a definite and determined movement to reinterpret the
ideals of Christian marriage to our young people;

Third, that we reaffirm both the sacredness of an individual's
religious faith in which both the husband and wife must be
equally free and that a fundamental tenet of our faith is violated

[4] Resolution of the American Baptist Convention, Boston, May, 1950.

if either the husband or wife is forced to sign away the religion of unborn children;

Fourth, that we further urge our young people to refuse to enter upon such agreements and steadfastly to maintain their own religious freedom and guarantee the religious freedom of their children.[5]

DISCIPLES OF CHRIST

Whereas, Mutual religious convictions, a common philosophy of life, and a similarity of cultural backgrounds are factors which contribute to a happy marriage; and

Whereas, Mutual respect for and sincere tolerance of differences on the part of both persons entering the union are indispensable, so that marriage can be a union of equals; and

Whereas, Some religious bodies (notably the Roman Catholic church) officially forbid their adherents to enter marriage with non-adherents except on the condition that non-adherents subscribe to certain agreements, particularly that the children of such a union be trained in the faith of the adherent, which in effect destroys any basis for tolerance and equality;

Whereas, Failure to understand and adequately to appreciate the implications of such agreements, before mutual attachment makes objective evaluation impossible, frequently leads later to disillusionment, family conflict and heartbreak;

Therefore, Be It *Resolved,* That this international Convention of Disciples of Christ urge parents, ministers and leaders of young people to provide in the home, in the church and through the normal channels of the teaching program instruction that will help youth, before or as they arrive at the age of forming intimate friendship between the sexes, to understand and appreciate the divergent interpretations relative to marriage held by different religious bodies; and further

Be It *Resolved,* That we request our young people to seek an understanding of the principles which underlie their Christian faith, to give prayerful consideration when faced with a situation where their wedding vows would entail agreements disparaging their basic Christian beliefs; and further

[5] Resolution of the Southern Baptist Convention, San Francisco, June, 1951 (item 102 of the minutes).

Be It *Resolved,* That we urge our young people to stand on their rights as self-respecting Christians, and that in no event they enter into a marriage contract which places them in a position of disadvantage in their family relationship and in the training of their children.[6]

JEWISH (REFORM)[7]

The Central Conference of American Rabbis declares that mixed marriages[8] are contrary to the tradition of the Jewish religion and should therefore be discouraged by the American rabbinate.[9]

LUTHERAN CHURCH—MISSOURI SYNOD

Whereas, Mixed marriages have become quite common among our people and

Whereas, Roman law pertaining to marriages between Lutherans and Roman Catholics requires instruction from a priest and/or the signing of the Roman prenuptial contract, and

Whereas, Said contract involves a sinful promise or oath; violates the Christian conscience; condemns unborn children to the soul-destroying religion of the Antichrist; and is diametrically opposed to the eternal truths of God; and

Whereas, The Word of God demands that every sin be warned against and that every willful transgression be dealt with; and

Whereas, There is a lack of uniformity of practice in dealing with mixed marriages between our membership and the Roman Catholic Church, and

Whereas, Continued inaction and a spirit of indifference will lead to confusion and dissension, therefore be it

Resolved, that we plead with our pastors and congregations to deal with this matter in their respective congregations in a firm, evangelical manner, and

[6] Resolution approved by the International Convention of Disciples of Christ, October, 1950, Oklahoma City, Oklahoma.

[7] The bodies representing the Orthodox and Conservative rabbinates have not adopted official statements, but rabbis of these persuasions will in fact not perform mixed marriages.

[8] As distinguished from "intermarriages" where the gentile party embraces Judaism.

[9] Resolution of the Central Conference of American Rabbis, 1909; reaffirmed in 1947.

Resolved, that we ask the Family Life Committee to provide our people with pertinent information as soon as possible.[10]

LUTHERAN, UNITED

No synodical action has been taken. Available, however, is a thorough report entitled *A Study of Mixed Marriages in the United Lutheran Church in America.*[11]

METHODIST

Religious convictions should be a strong tie in marriage. Recent research has emphasized the importance of common cultural and religious background as the foundation of successful marriage. It is therefore strongly urged that each young person consider carefully before becoming engaged to anyone who does not have a similar religious background. It is important that Protestant youth discuss this problem with their ministers before it is too late. Ministers are urged to discuss with both youth and parents the likelihood of failure in mixed marriages.[12]

The General Board of Education of The Methodist Church has issued a film on Roman Catholic-Protestant marriages entitled *One Love—Conflicting Faiths.*[13]

PRESBYTERIAN, UNITED

The Presbyterian Church in the U.S.A. today warned its members against contracting marriages with Roman Catholics, particularly when such marriages involve a promise to educate children in the Roman Catholic faith.

The warning was in a form of a resolution presented to the church's 162nd General Assembly by its special commission on marriage and divorce. It was adopted by a unanimous voice vote of the more than 800 commissioners.

The assembly action followed word for word a resolution

[10] Resolution adopted in Convention by the Lutheran Church—Missouri Synod, Houston, Texas, June, 1953.

[11] Published by the Church's Board of Social Missions, 231 Madison Ave., New York 16, New York.

[12] From Resolution on the Christian Family adopted by the General Conference, 1960.

[13] Inquiry may be made from the Television Radio and Film Commission, 1525 McGarock Street, Nashville, Tenn.

adopted the previous year by the Triennial General Convention of the Protestant Episcopal Church (see page 92).[14]

In recommending approval, the marriage commissioners proposed that the Presbyterian church unite with the Protestant Episcopal church on the issue and thereby take its place with another great communion of the Holy Catholic church in stressing the principles of Christian democracy and religious freedom.

The resolution also called on "all ministers of the Presbyterian church to inform our people of this action in all its implications." [15]

PRESBYTERIAN IN U.S. (commonly called "Southern")

Pastoral Letter

Increasingly evident is the unwisdom of the marriage between Presbyterians and Roman Catholics.

While the Roman Catholic laity accept Presbyterians as fellow Christians, their priests do not recognize our ministry as valid or our Communion as a part of the Church of Christ. This creates a deep and wide gulf which at once appears in the marriage rite itself.

If a priest of the Roman Catholic Church performs the ceremony, the Presbyterian party to the marriage is required to promise to do nothing to change the faith of the Roman Catholic party; altho the Roman Catholic is expected by his Church to win the Presbyterian. Also the Presbyterian is required to sign away the unborn children to an ecclesiastical organization that will forever forbid them to worship with their parent in the Presbyterian Church.

We call upon our members to stand uncompromisingly in this matter, to resist resolutely this unfair demand and refuse to make such a promise, especially in an hour when they are not truly free but are under the emotional compulsion of romantic love. Having acted under that compulsion the non-Catholic henceforth lives under a promise which a conscientious Christian will find it increasingly difficult to observe without mental and spiritual strain, threatening the peace and stability of the home.

[14] Presbyterian Church of the U.S.A., General Assembly, 1950, Resolution #6.
[15] *New York Times,* May 23, 1950.

If, on the other hand, a Presbyterian minister officiates at the marriage, the Roman Catholic party is denied the Communion of his Church and is considered by that Church to be living in sin.

Priding herself upon the rigid enforcement of her law the Roman Catholic Church is relentless in this matter, with the result that there has been, and is suffering and tragedy in many homes throughout our land.

In view of these facts, the General Assembly counsels Presbyterians to refrain from marriage with Roman Catholics as long as the demands and rulings of that church remain unchanged. This counsel is not given in a spirit of retaliation, even though we believe the demands and rulings mentioned to be harsh and unfair. We do not advance the cause of Christ by returning evil for evil. Positive and constructive action is demanded of us for the spiritual welfare of our people. The Roman Catholic attitude with reference to mixed marriages makes it impossible for a wholesome family religious life to exist and continually requires the Protestant to surrender or compromise his personal convictions. What is even more serious, it involves the signing away of the spiritual birthright of unborn children by denying them the possibility of any religious training in the home other than that prescribed by the Roman Catholic Church. It is far better that the parties concerned should not marry than that these tragic results should follow.[16]

In regard to marriage and the home. "The Catholic Church's attitude towards mixed marriages may be summed up briefly," writes Rev. John O'Conner, S.J., in a syndicated article for the Catholic press. "She strongly disapproves of them and strives to dissuade her children from contracting them." But that does not go to the heart of the matter. The non-Catholic who wants to marry a Catholic must promise in writing before a priest "that the non-Catholic will not interfere in the religious beliefs or practices of the Catholic party to the marriage; that all the children of the union will be baptized and reared in the Catholic faith."

Such a policy brings a heavy pressure to bear upon a young Protestant at a time when he is not able to exercise the clearest judgment and induces him to make a vow which is wrong at

[16] Minutes of the General Assembly of the Presbyterian Church, U.S., 1946, p. 165.

are frequently not limited to parents
the wider circles of the family. If
ers is sincere and strong, as it should
same warmth and fullness of kinship
respect for sincerely held convictions
e faith.

laim of the Roman Catholic Church
, as implied in the provisions of the
religion a divisive force in the family
d of unity and allegiance, as intended
y a home in which one party is as
other is assumed to be wrong has
in the building of enduring mutua
Such difficulties help to explain wh
xed marriages end in divorce as whe
e faith.

not surrender their faith lightly; an
ey will also do well to ask whether
the conditions imposed by the Roma
a sound spiritual basis for happy an
ss one himself believes in the Roma
Christianity firmly enough to becom
erent of that faith *before* marryin
ibed by the Roman Catholic Churcl
unborn children to a faith that he car
. It is equally wrong to withhold fror
om and joy of direct access to God.
ed to be on guard against two fals
oblems raised by mixed marriages. On
lightly or to subscribe to it with menta
responsible acts in the sight of God
ntal reservation that one does not in
is dishonest. It does not constitute
created by the conditions imposed b

the parties to a mixed marriage to fal
ous indifference. A right relationshij
of our lives. It is certainly not attained

the time, and which, if he understands the meaning of his Protestant faith, may become an intolerable one. Many pastors know
of the agony through which some of their members have gone as a
result. It is an open question whether one is morally obligated to
keep a vow which one has made under a type of duress, and which
comes to be regarded as contrary to the religious conscience. . . .
[Here follows a discussion of legal aspects of the antenuptial
agreement. See Chapter V.][17]

REFORMED

There is no synodical resolution of the Reformed Church in
America, but the matter is covered in a pamphlet on family counseling issued by the Church's Christian Action Commission.[18]

UNITED CHURCH OF CANADA

It is recommended that:

(1) The United Church of Canada re-affirm the historic position of the Christian Church in discouraging mixed marriages, in
principle:

(2) Our ministers counsel young people who contemplate contracting a mixed marriage to refuse to sign any document that
would alienate their right to be spiritual guides to their own
children or that would reflect on the validity of their own church
membership;

(3) The Federal Council of Churches pamphlet entitled, "If
I Marry a Roman Catholic," be put in the hands of any United
Church member contemplating a mixed marriage.

(4) The Commission on the Christian Faith be requested to
prepare a manual of Protestant doctrine, including a declaration
of belief, for the use of Roman Catholics who intend to marry
Protestants.[19]

UNITED CHURCH OF CHRIST

The Church of Jesus Christ has the solemn responsibility to teach
each new generation God's holy purpose for marriage, to estab-

[17] Minutes of the General Assembly, Presbyterian Church, U.S., 1948,
p. 160(2).

[18] 475 Riverside Drive, New York 27, N.Y.

[19] Record of Proceedings, General Council, United Church of Canada,
Montreal, 1946, p. 145.

lish the conditions so far as possible for its realization, and to warn against the dangers which threaten it. That purpose has been clearly disclosed in the words of our Lord: "From the beginning of creation, 'God made them male and female.' 'For this reason a man shall leave his father and mother and be joined to his wife, and the two shall become one.' So they are no longer two but one. What therefore God has joined together, let no man put asunder" (Mark 10:6–9).

The Apostle Paul has affirmed the sanctity and defined the character of the union of man and wife by comparing that union to the relation of Christ and his church: "Husbands, love your wives, as Christ loved the church and gave himself up for her. . . . For no man ever hates his own flesh, but nourishes and cherishes it, as Christ does the church, because we are members of his body" (Ephesians 5:25, 29 f.).

It is abundantly clear that the realization of God's purpose for married life—like every relation of Christian people to each other and to their fellow men—is grounded in and sustained by a sincere faith in God and a constant devotion to Christ and his church. The marriage relation is strengthened and sanctified when both man and wife meet the joys and sorrows, the stresses and strains, the successes and disappointments of their lives with a shared Christian faith and worship.

Marriages between Christians and non-Christians, therefore, present obvious obstacles to the realization in marriage of the full purpose of God. Even marriage between Protestant and Roman Catholic Christians involves difficulties arising out of different and partly incompatible interpretations of Christian truth. Because such a marriage puts obstacles in the way of realizing a union that can be compared to the union of Christ and his church, we call attention to the problems involved.

Both the Roman Catholic and the Protestant churches have been aware that difficulties exist. The Roman Church has devised and used an "antenuptial contract" as one means of dealing with so-called "mixed marriages"—marriages between a Roman Catholic and a non-Roman Catholic. Protestant churches have avoided the use of such a device as something alien to the character of Protestantism.

The marriage of a Roman Catholic to a Protestant Christian

children. The consequence and children, but extend religious faith in both part be, there can scarcely be th as when there is a mutua or when both are of the sa

In mixed marriages, the to be the only true churc antenuptial contract, make rather than the greatest bo by Almighty God. Certai sumed to be right while t great handicap to overcom esteem, harmony, and lov more than twice as many both parties are of the sa

Protestant Christians w they ought not to do so. marriage entered into und Catholic Church provide successful family life. Un Catholic interpretation o an honest and sincere under the conditions pre it is wrong to commit one not wholeheartedly embr them the Protestant's fre

Protestant Christians ways of escape from the false way is to take any v reservations. All vows a Taking a vow with the tend to fulfill his promi "solution" of the difficult the Church of Rome.

A second false way is into an attitude of reli with God is the chief er by indifference to God.

The following guiding principles are suggested as helpful:

1. Pastors and lay leaders should consider it a special duty to assist every confirmand and member to gain an intelligent understanding of the positive teachings of Protestant Christianity and of the essential differences between that and Roman Catholicism.

2. Parents and local church leaders should co-operate in counseling with youth concerning the problems involved in interfaith marriages during times of friendship, dating, and courtship.

3. Our young people should be helped to understand that marriages whether performed by Protestant or Roman Catholic clergy are valid in law and before God; and that the superior authority claimed by the Roman clergy and stressed by the Roman Church is an usurpation of the authority which belongs to Christ alone.

Since equal freedom of action is a requisite for mutuality in love and affection, people of different faiths are more likely to effect godly marriages through Protestant rites in which this freedom is kept inviolate than through Roman Catholic rites which deprive one of the contracting parties of freedom where this is most essential.

The response God asks of us is a response freely given. And in His service we find our freedom. To deny spiritual freedom to others is a grave offense. Hence the effort to restrict by "contracts" the freedom of persons—and, much more, the Spirit of God—is mistaken and wrong. We testify to our conviction that it is by placing ourselves under the Word of God and by being guided by the Holy Spirit who leads us into all truth that we find Him who is the Way and the Truth and the Life.[20]

[20] Statement adopted by the General Synod of the Evangelical and Reformed Church, 1953, and published by the United Church of Christ (a recent merger of the Evangelical and Reformed Church and the Congregational Churches).

❦

CHAPTER VII

A SUMMARY OF THE PROBLEM—
AND THE SOLUTION

SUFFICIENT HAS BEEN SAID to suggest the idea that a mixed marriage is not a good thing. Let us proceed briefly to summarize why:

1. A mixed marriage lacks a commonly held and articulated basis of ideas, purposes, and motivations.

2. A mixed marriage lacks the resources of marital health provided by common worship and common involvement in the most significant of all possible interests.

3. A mixed marriage robs the parents of a common relationship with their children on the deepest level, namely of spiritual life.

4. In a mixed marriage one of the parents—and sometimes both—are robbed of the opportunity of bringing to their children the best spiritual heritage that he or she knows, being barred from discharging this most important aspect of parental responsibility.

5. A mixed marriage (if one of the parties is a Roman Catholic) disenables one of the parties from following his conscience in regard to the planning of parenthood.

THE "COMMON IDEALS" SOLUTION

As devastating as all of these factors—when marshaled—may look to an outsider, they may well not be strong enough to down the hopes of those whose love is strong and genuine. So there is generally a "last-ditch" improvisation designed to present a hopeful prospect. This particular improvisation is heard on the lips of "mixed" couples of all types.

> *Case 16.* We have plenty of common ground under our feet: We have our love, we have our ideals; we know what we want out of life, we think that we can bring fine things to our children. And all this though we are of different religions.

Taking this doubtless sincere statement at its face value, what it really means is this: We have a common religion, the particular religious labels we bear are secondary to us. Though the couple might find difficulty in stating what these "ideals" are, difficulty in defining what the purposes of life are, if they really mean that Roman Catholicism, Presbyterianism, Judaism, or what not, is not to be the guiding norm of their lives nor the heritage given their children, then there are several important questions for them to consider: Is the new religion which they have invented ("our ideals," "our purposes," "fine things") really profound and meaningful, and will it abide not only during the sunny periods of life but during the crises? In adopting a view of life which is in effect a rejecting or subordination of their own religious heritages, do they have a really better way of life than these heritages represent? In what religious ceremony for their marriage and with what continuity of worship during their marriage (and with their children) will they appropriately express and deepen these convictions?

THE TRUE SOLUTION

In most cases these questions cannot be answered satisfactorily. But nevertheless in the rebellion which this attitude expresses, and in their desire to do something new and creative in order

to provide a common basis for the marriage, the couple is feeling after what is in fact the true solution, and it is the purpose
of this chapter to present this solution.

Let us first begin by asking this question: Why are people
what they are religiously? More often than not people are what
they are because of what they were born. Now of all the reasons to hold to a particular religious faith this is the least convincing. Actually it would have been quite possible for the
couple under consideration to have been born "totem-pole"
worshipers: the fact that they were born such would not prove
the validity of their position. The fact that one's parents are
of a particular religious faith proves little also. One's parents
can be wrong—and in fact most people of marriageable age
have already decided that their parents are wrong in a number
of particulars. So why not religiously? This is a good question
to ask under any circumstances as a young person approaches
adult life, but it is an especially good question to ask at the
time of marriage. For now a new unit of society is being created and one which will be autonomous to a considerable degree. In the Bible which Roman Catholics and other Christians alike read is this word: "A man shall leave father or
mother and cleave to his wife." Next to God and one's religious loyalty, loyalty to one's spouse is the first loyalty. Parents
come second; and after the children are born, the children
come second and the parents are third in the priority scale of
allegiance. (Were this a general book on marriage counseling
this point would be stressed for several pages.)

The solution, in a nutshell, is this: each of the parties, forgetting what he or she was born and forgetting what his parents are, should rethink his or her religious position in terms
of what each really believes and what Church most nearly represents that actual belief. Naturally the religious allegiances in
which the two are now actually involved should be given serious consideration in the study, but the search need not be
limited to them. If it so happens that both parties can come
to convictions which are represented by the same Church al-

legiance then there will be no mixed marriage. And that is the end of the problem.

It is important at the outset to state what the above paragraph does *not* mean. It does not mean that one should seek to persuade himself of the truth of the other's position or yield to it in order to simplify things. This is to make one of the parties into an adjective and leave the other a noun, and in fact to deify one of the two parties. This subjugation of the spirit of one to the other is bound to have difficult psychological consequences in all aspects of the marriage—beyond the question of religion proper. If, however, this honest reconsideration leads both to conviction as to a faith that happens to be already that of one of the two parties, both should have the humility to make possible the conversion of the heretofore outsider to this faith without any sense of having "yielded" to the other. In no case should one yield to the other; both should yield to the claims of truth as they have worked it out through honest study, soul searching and decision. Any other solution does violence to the integrity of one or the other of the parties. Too easy a victory here will be paid for in the end.

The problem for mixed marriages in which one of the parties is a Roman Catholic—to put it in the most painful but blunt manner—is this: If the non-Roman party declines to sign the antenuptial agreement and the marriage is performed by other than a Roman Catholic priest, the Roman Catholic is excommunicated and loses his religious *pou sto*. If the Protestant party does sign the promises he has ridden over his own religious allegiance roughshod, has committed a serious sin because of this decision not to exercise his primary responsibility toward his children, has put himself in the position of finding it very difficult to repent (and properly amend) his action. While his church may not "excommunicate" him in a formal sense, he should feel barred from communion with God— through the sacrament or otherwise—until he can work out some solution as to the matter of repentance of sin. So in essence both parties are in the same situation, or, to put it in another way, one of the parties is in a fix either way the matter is decided.

Though the problem is not so acute in the case of other types of mixed marriages, with different nomenclature much the same dilemma is presented.

At this point some people throw up their hands and utter such clichés as "A Catholic can never become a non-Catholic!" Such statements as this don't really hold water because they mean either "I don't care about the truth of it, I like the feel of it," or "My religion is right because I hold it." Furthermore it overlooks the obvious fact that all through history and at the present day many intelligent people have through conviction changed their religious allegiances: and no church can claim a one-way traffic in its direction.[1]

Nothing but good can come from this approach to things. If as a result of careful study of his own tradition and of the principal alternatives a person decides to stay put, then it is obvious that he will henceforth have a much more mature faith and reasoned allegiance than he had before. On the other hand, if he decides to change his new allegiance such a change will be on the dignified basis of adult conviction, not on the basis which is so destructive of personal integrity: the yielding of one's loyalties because of the other partner in the marriage.

---

[1] A survey conducted by *The Christian Herald* (April, 1954) indicated that over four million Roman Catholics became members of other Christian bodies in the United States in a period of ten years. The official *Catholic Directory* for 1953 indicated that there were over a million adult converts to the Roman Catholic Church during the same period.

A sexennial survey of United Lutheran congregations (released by the National Lutheran Council on March 23, 1954) indicates approximately this same ratio, i.e., that four times as many Roman Catholics became United Lutherans as vice versa.

A statistical study made in 1949 showed that about 4,000 Roman Catholics were becoming Episcopalians every year and estimated the favorable ratio as to the two-way traffic higher than the later studies cited above (*Living Church*, September 19, 1950).

The first and third of these studies were criticized by Roman Catholic spokesmen. But regardless of the precise accuracy of any one of these studies, they certainly do indicate that people *do* change—and both ways—which is our point here.

THE SPIRIT OF THE INQUIRY

Nothing could be more important than the spirit with which any such study is undertaken. If one party has entered it in good faith and the other has in mind only "to bring around" his partner, this attitude will become evident enough during the process and will have either the result of "putting off" the latter or of bullying him into submission. Naturally no one can be expected to be suspended religiously in mid-air in order to give objective consideration to all other possibilities; no one can be asked to forego his regular worship or his normal prayer life or the particular obligations imposed upon him by his own church while he examines the historical and theological foundations of his practices, and of their alternatives. If a family has decided to consider where in the community they would best like to live, life still goes on as usual in the old house, though the latter may be undergoing a more critical and systematic examination than would be customary.

Nor is there any thought that emotions should be ruled out. One's attraction to, antagonism toward, or intuitions about, particular religious teachings or practices are part of what eventually should be weighed in the balance. However, the human emotions are capable of great resiliency. We are capable of wider attractions than we realize; when we know the background and reason for a particular attitude or custom we often find that it is more attractive than we had imagined it could be. The same is true of the breadth of our antagonisms. When we allow what have often been suppressed resentments to come to the surface in the course of our survey of religious possibilities, we often find that we have not been as totally satisfied with our own tradition as we have claimed we have been.

Case 17. When the subject of their religious differences came up, one of the first things Mary, a Roman Catholic, said to John, an Episcopalian, was: "I could never do without the Mass, and of course your church doesn't have that."

But the first time she attended a choral celebration of the Holy Communion (the same service which the Roman Catholic Church calls "High Mass") in an Episcopal church she found in fact that she felt quite at home and as a matter of fact rejoiced at the fact that the service was in her own language, commenting, "I had always wondered if it wouldn't be better if our service was in English; and I am frank to say that I like it that way better; I like the way the congregation all took part."

Case 18. A constant source of irritation to Bill had been the fact that his Roman Catholic friends had to get to Mass on Sunday come what may. Now in the course of his instructions from a Roman Catholic priest he is beginning to look at the thing "from the inside." He sees the point of such a rule and as a matter of fact finds himself highly critical of the laissez-faire attitude toward discipline of this sort which has been evidenced in his own Church.

Case 19. Of a strong Baptist background, Florence has never had any use for symbolism, vestments, or ceremony. But now that she has started to go to the Lutheran Church on alternate Sundays with Walter, who has carefully explained the various usages of his church, she finds these externals both beautiful and helpful to worship. She finds to her surprise that a fixed order of worship can make for more congregational participation, rather than less, as she had supposed.

Case 20. William, an agnostic of long standing, had always assumed that belief in the Divinity of Christ depended upon accepting the Virgin Birth—an idea to which he had a closed mind. Mary's minister explained to him that there were good grounds for accepting the Incarnation quite apart from the Virgin Birth, that many people who accepted the former did not regard the latter as essential, except as a mode of expressing the former. Thus this barrier to belief was removed. As he began to participate in worship, he found the phrase "conceived by the Holy Ghost, born of the Virgin Mary" quite appropriate to recite in the Creed as a way of expressing the Incarnation. Finally he came up with this idea one day: "It is such a good way to say it, maybe it was a good way for God to do it."

These illustrations should be sufficient to rebut the notion expressed in such statements as "but I could never . . ." or "I'll always . . ."

THE METHOD OF INQUIRY

How shall a couple proceed to learn about the major alternatives? The tragedy of the education (high school or college) of most young people is that it has not included a systematic study of the major traditions in religion. To know these things is simply part of being an educated person, yet due to the secularization of public education and, until recently, of most higher education, most people approach adult life religiously illiterate. This means that the couple in question must now proceed to complete their own education. Customary educational methods are relevant in this connnection.

First, it is important to talk to professionals devoted to the alternative positions. As we have seen, the Roman Catholic Church has already made provision for this aspect of the study. It generally requires of a non-Roman party instructions in the Roman Catholic faith. Normally the Roman Catholic party will attend also. Often the non-Roman party (and sometimes the Roman Catholic party) resents this rule. Actually it is a quite reasonable requirement. The difficulty is that it is usually not "fifty-fifty." To provide for this aspect of the study we need only to take what is now common practice as to the Roman Catholic side, and extend it to the other alternative: sessions should be arranged with a minister or other spokesman of that position also.

Meanwhile, the couple should be doing some reading to-

gether. Every religious tradition has provided some pamphlets
and books which expound its attitudes and provide a rationale
for its positions. The priest, minister, or other adviser may well
be able to suggest these books and pamphlets. Here we set
forth a selected bibliography providing a few informative books
for each of the principal religious traditions, arranged in alpha-
betical order:

BAPTIST (NORTHERN)

Ralph M. Johnson and R. Dean Goodwin, *Faith, Functions,
Fellowship of American Baptists* (Judson Press, 1951)
Henry K. Rose, *The Baptist Witness* (Judson Press, 1951)
Hillyer H. Straton, *The Baptists: Their Message and Mission*
(Judson Press, 1951)

BAPTIST (SOUTHERN)

James E. Dillard, *We Southern Baptists* (Executive Committee,
Southern Baptist Convention, Nashville, Tenn., revised edi-
tion 1948–1949)
W. W. Barnes, *The Southern Baptist Convention, 1845–1953*
(Broadman Press, 1954)

CHRISTIAN SCIENTIST

Mary Baker Eddy, *Science and Health with Key to the Scrip-
tures—Christian Scientist Textbook* (Horace J. Carver, 1910)
Mary Baker Eddy, *Rudimental Divine Science* (Horace J.
Carver, 1908)

DISCIPLES OF CHRIST

Winfred Garrison, *An American Religious Movement* (Chris-
tian Board of Publication, 1945)
Howard E. Short, *Doctrine and Thought of the Disciples of
Christ* (Christian Board of Publication, 1951)

EASTERN ORTHODOX

Nicholas Zernov, *Church of the Eastern Christians* (S.P.C.K.,
1948)
Frank Gavin, *Greek Orthodox Thought* (Morehouse-Gorham,
1923)

Michael Constantinides, *The Orthodox Church* (Greek Theological Seminary, 1952)

The following book is more specifically concerned with comparison with, and critique of, Roman Catholicism:

A. Kokkinakis, *Christian Orthodoxy and Roman Catholicism* (Greek Archdiocese of North and South America, 1952)

EPISCOPAL

George Hodges, *The Episcopal Church* (Morehouse-Gorham, 1938)

James A. Pike and W. Norman Pittenger, *The Faith of the Church* (Seabury Press, 1951)

Massey R. Shepherd, *The Worship of the Church* (Seabury Press, 1952)

ETHICAL CULTURE

Felix Adler, *An Ethical Philosophy of Life* (Appleton-Century-Crofts, 1918)

David S. Muzzey, *Ethics as a Religion* (Simon & Schuster, 1951)

JEWISH

Will Herberg, *Judaism and Modern Man* (Jewish Publication Society, 1951)

Milton Steinberg, *Basic Judaism* (Harcourt, Brace & Co., 1949)

Philip S. Bernstein, *What the Jews Believe* (Farrar, Straus & Young, 1950)

Morris Kertzer, *What Is a Jew?* (World Publishing Co., 1952)

LUTHERAN

Stanley E. Carnarius, *What Lutherans Believe* (United Lutheran Publication House, 1951)

Eric H. Wahlstrom, *The Church and the Means of Grace* (Augustana Book Concern, 1951)

Amos J. Traver, *A Lutheran Handbook* (Muhlenberg Press, 1949)

W. E. Schramm, *What Lutherans Believe* (Wartburg Press, 1946)

METHODIST

Discipline of the Methodist Church (Methodist Publishing House, 1952)

Clinton Cherry, *The Beliefs of a Methodist Christian* (Tidings. 1949)

Paul B. Kern, *Methodism Has a Message* (Abingdon Press, 1941)

PRESBYTERIAN

James Smart, *What a Man Can Believe* (Westminster Press, 1943)

George Sweazey, *The Christian Answer to Life's Urgent Problems* (Hink House, 1950)

John Calvin, *A Compend of the Institutes of the Christian Religion* (Westminster Press, 1939)

W. T. Hanzsche, *Know Your Church* (Westminster Press, 1946)

Clifford M. Drury, *Presbyterian Panorama* (Board of Christian Education of the Presbyterian Church, 1952)

PROTESTANT (in general)

James H. Nichols, *Primer for Protestants* (Association Press, 1950)

Harry C. Munro, *Be Glad You're a Protestant* (Bethany Press, 1948)

S. Burnet Easton, *Faith of a Protestant* (Macmillan, 1946)

James A. Pike, *The Things Most Surely Believed Among Us* (National Council of Churches of Christ, 1951)

The following books are more specifically concerned with comparisons with, and critique of, Roman Catholicism:

C. P. S. Clarke, *The Roman Claims* (A. R. Mowbray & Co., 1951)

Richard Hanson and Reginald Fuller, *The Church of Rome: A Dissuasive* (S. C. M. Press, 1948)

Kenneth N. Ross, *Why I Am Not a Roman Catholic* (A. R. Mowbray & Co., 1953)

William S. Kerr, *Handbook on the Papacy* (Philosophical Library, 1931)

The following are concerned with the problem of mixed marriages from the Protestant point of view:

If I Marry a Roman Catholic (Joint Department of Family Life, National Council of Churches, 1945)

Benjamin Lotz, *An Un-American Marriage,* reprinted from *The Christian Century* (Wartburg Press, 1944)

QUAKER (FRIENDS)

Rufus M. Jones, *Faith and Practice of the Quakers* (London, 1927)

Quaker Message, compiled by Sidney Lucas (Pendle Hill, 1948)

William Wistar Comfort, *Quakers in the Modern World* (New York, 1949)

REFORMED (DUTCH)

Howard Hageman, *Our Reformed Church* (Half Moon Press, 1952)

Howard Hageman, *Lily Among the Thorns* (Half Moon Press, 1953)

ROMAN CATHOLIC

John G. Brunini, *Whereon to Stand* (Harper & Brothers, 1946)

Karl Adam, *The Spirit of Catholicism* (Macmillan Co., 1943)

John C. Heenan, *The Faith Makes Sense* (Sheed and Ward, 1948)

The following books are more specifically concerned with comparison with, and critique of, non-Roman Christianity:

Konrad Algermisse, *Christian Denominations* (B. Herder Book Co., 1945)

Robert Hugh Benson, *Non-Catholic Denominations* (Longmans Green, 1915)

Otto Karrer, *Religions of Mankind* (Sheed and Ward, 1945)

Rumble & Carthy, *Radio Replies,* Vol. II (Radio Replies Press, 1940)

John L. Stoddard, *Rebuilding a Lost Faith* (P. J. Kenedy, 1922)

The following are concerned with the problem of mixed marriages from the Roman Catholic point of view:

John C. Heenan, *They Made Me Sign* (Sheed and Ward, 1949)

John A. O'Brien, *The Truth About Mixed Marriages—What to Do About Them* (Our Sunday Visitor Press, 1953)

Seventh Day Adventist

A. S. Maxwell, *Your Friends, the Adventists* (Pacific Press Publishing Association, 1950)

C. B. Haynes, *Seventh Day Adventist's Work and Teaching* (Review and Herald Publishing Association, 1940)

Unitarian-Universalist

Earl Morse Wilbur, *Our Unitarian Heritage* (Beacon Press, 1925)

John Nicholls Booth, *Introducing Unitarianism* (American Unitarian Association, 1944)

Alfred Cole, *Hell's Ramparts Fell* (Murray Press, 1941)

Clarence Skinner, *Social Implications of Universalism* (Murray Press, 1915)

United Church of Christ

Gaius Glenn Atkins and Frederick L. Fagley, *History of American Congregationalism* (Pilgrim Press, 1942)

Walter M. Horton, *Our Christian Faith* (Pilgrim Press, 1945)

Paul T. Stonesifer, *Know Your Church* (Department of United Promotion of the Evangelical and Reformed Church, 1934)

My Church and I (issued by the Evangelical and Reformed Church, 1939)

KNOWING THE WAY OF WORSHIP

The third important element of the inquiry is actual experience in the worship of the several traditions under consideration. What is called for here is something halfway between a "balcony" attitude and the attitude of participation. One should make the responses called for in the particular liturgy, join in the prayers, sing the hymns and pray personally as one is being led in prayer by the clergyman. On the other hand, it is generally sensible for the visitor to be alert and observant as to what is going on and be critically related to it. In short it would be wrong to come to a service of worship with an attitude which can be summed up as "I dare you to convert me" or with a determination to try and like it regardless. To achieve the proper in-between attitude is, by the way, a very important test of maturity.

Case 21. Lydia, a Protestant, is attending her first Roman Catholic Mass with her friend, Joseph. He has handed her a missal with an English translation, but she is so fascinated with all that she sees around her that she takes refuge in the fact that practically all of the Roman Catholics present are not using missals but are saying the Rosary and reading devotional prayer books, and thus does not feel called upon to follow her missal. As a result she comes away with a feeling that the whole thing was a rather confusing experience. Actually it would have been fairer for her to have operated on the best level to which the Roman Catholic Church is seeking to bring its own people—namely, the use of a missal, which allows the worshiper to follow the service with the priest and choir.

Case 22. Helen, a former Roman Catholic who is now an agnostic, is attending an Episcopal service with Jim. Though the *Agnus Dei* is usually sung during the Communion at the Episcopal service, a hymn (which the Prayer Book permits) was used in this particular parish. "Where was the *Agnus Dei?*" she whispers critically to Jim. Helen, away from the Roman Catholic Church for some years, still uses the Roman Catholic Mass, which is familiar to her, as the norm for all true worship. Actually she does not realize that the *Agnus Dei* was a quite late addition to the Latin Mass.

In selecting places of worship an opportunity should be given for the best of each tradition to present itself. It is not fair to compare a High Mass sung in a rural "carpenter's gothic" Roman Catholic church with choral Eucharist in an Episcopal church with a large music budget, soaring arches and the finest stained glass; nor a small-town Congregational service with a Park Avenue Methodist church with a distinguished preacher. In any case a certain degree of generalization is called for. The couple should not be basing their judgment on the local church as such, but only on what the church or denomination as a whole represents. For what they will be giving their loyalty to is not a particular parish or congregation but to a world communion with a particular tradition.

Finally, discussion between the two parties is of great importance. The degree to which they can in this situation maintain objectivity, candor, and a sense of humor is a good test of the way they are apt to conduct their marriage. After an exceptionally poor sermon in the other party's church (*any* church—no denomination has a monopoly on this), the proper remark is not "Well, that's a point for my side, dear," but rather "I am sure *that* preaching is a purely local problem." In discussing points of doctrine or church history, the attitude should not be, how much can I rebut? but how much can I concede, with honesty? When a common ground is found on some things and differences on others, even then a deadlock is not to be declared. Some consideration should be given as to what other alternatives than those already considered offer affirmation of this common ground along with the particular other points which each of the parties feel should receive expression.

Case 23. Very important to Christopher, a Congregationalist, is a liberal attitude toward the Scriptures and certain Reformation principles such as the direct relationship of the individual to God and the place of the laity in the government of the Church. Very important to Marie, a Roman Catholic, is the Holy Communion and a traditional order of worship. Both agree on the basic essentials of the Christian faith. Their friends suggested that they look into the Episcopal Church. It so happened that there each felt he found what he was looking for, and the decision was not a compromise (as a sort of "middle" or *via media*) but rather was the fulfillment of what each regarded as most important in religion, with ample room for what the other regarded as important. Three years later we find Marie especially gratified at the liberal attitude toward the Scriptures and the other Reformation principles which were dear to Christopher; and especially dear to Christopher is the Eucharist and an ordered liturgy.

In this chapter we have outlined the separate elements of the proper kind of consideration of alternative traditions. However, these particular methods need not fall strictly in this order. Consultation, reading, worship and discussion should all go ahead at once. Reading will lead to further consultation, as will worship. Discussion will lead to the need of further reading, etc. If the right spirit is present (along the lines we discussed above) and there is true respect between the parties, here we *can* affirm that "love will find a way." Negatively speaking, this much can be said: If in this most important realm of relationships, this kind of open dealing is impossible and if already we sense a dogmatic sense of rightness on one person's part and a "looking down the nose" at the other party's tradition, we can already sense the beginning of second-rate citizenship for one of the partners to the marriage—and the parties had better beware of the perils of the future.

A SPECIAL PROBLEM FOR ROMAN CATHOLICS

Before closing the chapter, we should give consideration to a special problem which arises when one of the parties to the mutual consideration of the faiths is a Roman Catholic. The Roman Catholic Church endorses the procedure here outlined —except they endorse it as a one-way matter only. They are very happy to have the non-Roman party take instruction from a Roman Catholic priest, attend services, read assigned books. They are also happy to have the Roman Catholic party co-operate in expounding the faith to the non-Roman party (in fact that the Roman Catholic party will try to do this is one of the promises he signs in the antenuptial agreement). In all of this they are very sound; no right-thinking Christian should take exception to such activity. The only difficulty is— and to this anyone on the outside can properly take exception —they do not invite the Roman party to make a similar study of other traditions. Indeed they forbid the same. The Roman Catholic is forbidden by his church to read books on religion written by non-Romans, and is forbidden to attend services of worship of other bodies. He is also forbidden to consult, on religious subjects, with a minister of religion other than a Roman Catholic priest.

Now here is a place where the clearest thinking is called for. It is not the purpose of this book to question the teachings or disciplines of any religious group, or to provide arguments for or against them. However, it is necessary to point out that if we are to have a type of weighing and balancing with which this chapter is concerned, one of the issues at stake (where one of the parties is a Roman Catholic) is the authority of the Roman Catholic Church. If indeed the Pope is infallible and the Roman Catholic Church is the true Church, its confining disciplines should be followed to the letter. But the very question to be decided, in this case, is whether or not the Pope *is* infallible and whether or not the Roman Catholic Church *is* the only true Church. A Roman Catholic, especially one who has been born such, and who has given no independent study to the positions contrary to this view, and to the positive convictions and bases of authority proposed by other traditions, *is not dealing fairly* with the other party, who, we will assume, is quite willing to consider the claims of the Roman Catholic Church seriously and to take instructions from a Roman Catholic priest, *if* he is not willing to reciprocate, and give fair and objective consideration to the other principal alternatives to his own faith.

The result of this process may of course be a deeper conviction in his Roman Catholicism. Well and good—whatever that may mean as to the proposed marriage. In this case, he would be all the more inclined to put his religious loyalty ahead of loyalty to the person, even the person he is in love with. And this is right; it is precisely what convinced adherents of any other religious tradition should do. But not to give thoroughgoing study, with all the best resources (which include consultation with theologically-trained representatives, reading of the best exponents, and experience of worship on the best level), is to fail to tender due respect to the deepest levels in the background and present make-up of the other party. And when this respect is lacking and co-operation missing even during the period of courtship, the other party can be sure that it will not be present in the years after marriage. I know of few non-Roman clergy who would fear to have their parishioners undertake a study of Roman Catholicism, and for that matter take instruction under a Roman Catholic priest, provided the matter is handled on a fifty-fifty basis and the couple comes to him for instruction as well. The fact that the Roman Catholic Church apparently fears this experience for its communicant should in itself raise a serious question in the minds of both parties.

Case 24. In their initial conference with Father Smith, Alfred and Jane are told that Alfred, a Protestant, will have to undergo instruction in the Roman Catholic faith. Alfred agrees and mentions that he will arrange instruction for Jane in the teaching of his Church. "But," counters Father Smith, "Jane will not be allowed to do this." Both Alfred and Jane sense the unfairness of this attitude and conclude the conference by saying that they will think about the whole matter. Because most American Roman Catholics are "infected" with general American (and Protestant) "fifty-fifty" notions of "fair play," they are sufficiently irritated by Father Smith's attitude to go the same evening to see Dr. Walters, Alfred's minister. "Before making your decision," said Dr. Walters, "I think it would be well if you both came to me for a series of conferences about the teaching of our church." "But I suppose," said Jane, "that you would be opposed to Alfred's taking instruction from my priest." "By no means;" Dr. Walters adds, "in fact I was going to recommend that you both take instruction in Roman Catholic teaching from your priest, Jane, because I imagine you are a little rusty on things yourself. Anyway, it is better for a couple to do these things together. That way their discussion afterward is a great deal more useful."

THE TIMING

A study of all religious possibilities could be a lifetime task. And, since long engagements are not favored these days, there will naturally be some limit upon the extent of this enterprise, important as it is. But we must remember that once the couple has gotten used to studying religion together, they will probably continue it after their marriage and have ample opportunity to learn about the many things they had not considered before they made their decision in face of the problem of mixed marriage. They may even eventually decide for another religious allegiance than the one in which they decided to be married. This is fine, if the decision is made on the basis of mature study and conviction which we have been here recommending. But looking toward the time of marriage some limits must be set to this activity, and the number of alternatives to be given serious consideration will have to be limited. Obviously the two traditions in which the couple find themselves should be given priority in attention, and along with them perhaps a couple of possibilities which, from the outside looking in, may strike them as "in-between" (though they may not decide so to characterize them after they study them).

It is well not to leave all of the deciding to the end. As the couple goes along in study and comparison, certain issues can be settled, certain common ground can be agreed upon, and certain issues delineated for further study, inquiry, and observation. In any case it is important that the decision not be made as a matter of "snap judgment," as an emotional reaction to what may seem to be an unreasonable priest or minister, an unattractive service or sermon, or an unconvincing book. Too much is at stake to allow petty feelings, momentary reactions and particular instances to play that large a part.

Sometimes, however, circumstances are such that the marriage is imminent. Perhaps the couple is facing the problem of the mixed marriage too late in their courtship. Perhaps some special circumstances—such as military duty—may require an early marriage. If so, it is important that the couple find a forum for the marriage which will not finally settle any issues and then resolve to enter upon the study of those suggested in the early days of the married life. When they have come to their conclusions they can then "fix up" the marriage along the proper lines.

Case 25. Jim and Esther were agnostics, although Jim had a nominal connection with the Episcopal Church. Impending naval duty for Jim advanced the time of marriage and there was neither the time nor the disposition to give serious study to the matter of the religious future of the household. Quite properly—under these circumstances, they were married by a judge. A year or so later, after they had been converted to the Christian faith and after considering several alternatives, they decided upon the Episcopal Church. Their marriage was then blessed by an Episcopal priest, at a simple service in the church.

Case 26. Fred, a Methodist, and Ruth, a Roman Catholic, have good reason to get married within the next two weeks. He is unwilling to sign the antenuptial agreement but is willing to give consideration, on a mutual basis, to the claims of the Roman Catholic Church. Unwilling to settle so important a problem in two weeks, Fred and Ruth decide to be married by a friend's minister (a Presbyterian), since no antenuptial agreement is required by his church, intending to give careful study to both alternatives, realizing full well that if they decide on the Roman Catholic Church they will have no difficulty in being remarried by a Roman Catholic priest (should Fred decide to become a Roman Catholic), and knowing that the marriage ceremony performed would be quite adequate should Ruth decide to become a Methodist.

THIS IS THE SOLUTION

No matter what the particular details as to timing and arrangements may be, the approach outlined in this chapter is the only one for two sincere people of different religious backgrounds who have respect for the integrity of each other's convictions and yet who recognize the impasse which a mixed marriage would involve. It is an impasse which allows neither party to be truly faithful to his convictions, and which requires one of the parties to be particularly unfaithful thereto. It results in a marriage leaving out too much that is basic and important for themselves and for the children. In any case the experience of mature consideration of various religious possibilities is an important one for the adult life of an individual. More often than not the couple in fact comes together in a common allegiance. After careful study, if they cannot, then it is well for them to know that these divergences do exist and they may well decide not to get married. Perhaps there are some circumstances where they should go ahead. But enough has been said in earlier chapters to raise a grave question about proceeding. Certainly if the parties are young, they would do well to wait until the opportunity comes for a marriage with a common religious undergirding.

CHAPTER VIII

JEWISH-CHRISTIAN MARRIAGES

ALL THAT HAS BEEN SAID before is applicable to the particular "mixture" to be discussed in this chapter, and in fact several examples of this type of intermarriage already have been used illustratively. In theory no special analysis is called for. But in practice special considerations enter the picture due to the intertwining of sociological, cultural and religious factors in Jewish-gentile relations and the widespread lack of precision with which these factors are dealt with in the thinking of people generally, and particularly by those involved in such a possible marriage—and by their relatives and friends.

This very confusion made it difficult to select a title for the chapter. For the non-Jewish party there are two words which can be used: "Christian" and "gentile"; "Jewish" is the opposite of both these words. And the two words "Christian" and "gentile" are often used interchangeably, improper as such usage may be. A minister of the author's acquaintance was interested in taking his vacation at a New England resort and he sent for some literature on it. In the brochure there was the phrase "Christian clientele only." To an enthusiastic letter he replied with a fine irony: "I have examined my conscience for some days, and I am not entirely sure that I qualify." Actually it is very unlikely that management cared a whit about the orthodoxy of his convictions, nor—except for the more obvious proprieties—the depth of his Christian ethics, nor the regularity of his churchgoing; they simply wanted to be sure that he wasn't a Jew.

The plain truth is that many who are distressed about the possibilities of a mixed marriage in this general category have only a secondary interest in the religious problem that may be involved—and in fact, as we shall see, there may be none involved. But the concern is often about the prospective crossing of the lines of social groupings within our culture—a division which is of course not a matter of race, but one of sociological origin (one cannot even say national origin, until the day comes that there are considerable numbers of emigrees from the new state of Israel). There is no intent here to minimize the role which such a factor can play in a marriage, nor the part that under certain circumstances it might play in the decision to marry; and some consideration will be given to this matter a little later on. But of first importance is the distinction between the religious and sociological issues, because the part each plays in the total situation requires a quite distinct analysis, and nothing but confusion results from the failure to deal with each of the problems on its own footing—whatever the ultimate outcome may be in a given case. Because the confusion on the two issues is usually compounded with prejudice—often from both sides of the fence, generally more heat than light is generated in family discussions on the subject.

Case 27. Mary has just announced her plans to marry David, who is of Jewish extraction. Her parents immediately protest that a mixed marriage is not a good idea. "We have always been a Christian family," says her father. "And just think what this will mean to your children." Mary's explanation that David has never so much as entered a synagogue and is not particularly interested in the Jewish religion does not in fact make her parents feel any better. Nor does it occur to them to take into account the fact that

Mary herself has not been to church for five years, having counted herself an agnostic since college days, nor the fact that they themselves have no active interest in the Christian Church.

The fact is, whatever may be the social problems involved, religiously speaking this proposed union is not a "mixed marriage" at all. It is a contemplated marriage between two modern young secularists, which stands on about the same religious footing as marriage between a lapsed Presbyterian and a lapsed Methodist.

Case 28. Let us assume that Mary goes further and explains that she and David have talked out the whole matter of religion and have decided that they had a sufficiently common set of principles—none of which requires any connection with a church—to work out a fine marriage, and that, as far as children are concerned, they will let them choose for themselves. The answer to these two variants of "But we'll find a way to work it out" have already been given earlier (Chapter IV). But the interesting point here is that parents who would be inclined to accept this analysis were her prospective fiancé named Reginald find it quite unconvincing under the circumstances.

In some instances the opposition is not relieved even when there is a prospect of solving the religious problem satisfactorily.

Case 29. Nathan and Josephine, a Jew and a Christian, go to Josephine's minister to talk the problem over. She is a serious Congregationalist and does in fact conceive of the problem in religious terms. The minister suggests that, since Nathan is in fact practicing no religion and Josephine is, he give a serious hearing to the claims of Christianity, and he proposes some reading. A second interview reveals that Nathan is considerably impressed and that he wants to go further with the discussions along this line. Her parents are regular church-going Congregationalists and normally would be pleased at word of such a possible conversion. But in fact they show no pleasure and, in addition to doubting the sincerity of Nathan, are pressed to articulate what is the real difficulty, the depth of which is only superficially—but yet tellingly—revealed by the comment of Josephine's mother: "But he wouldn't be welcome at the country club with us!"

The reaction of parents has been used in the illustration only to describe the confusion involved. But since members of the present generation are more likely to discount prejudice than their elders, and since independent decision about marriage is a more frequent occurrence these days, let us not assume that no one can see through this problem clearly, simply because many parents do not. First, we will analyze the religious issues involved, and then we will find that the cultural factors fall readily into perspective.

THE RELIGIOUS PROBLEM

Just as "Christian" designates anyone from a Bulgarian Orthodox to a Seventh Day Adventist, the word "Jewish" covers a wide scope of religious belief and practice. Thus no general conclusions can be drawn, in spite of our tendency to draw them due to the general intercultural and religious ignorance which prevails.

Religiously speaking, there are four kinds of Jews: Orthodox, Conservative, Reform and secularist.

We need not tarry on the subject of mixed marriages involving an Orthodox Jew, since it does not represent a very likely occurrence. Much more than almost any other tradition in our culture, Orthodox Judaism is a whole way of life, and one which separates its members from social contacts with gentiles which would be likely to lead to marriage, and provides strong group pressures against the apostasy involved in mixed marriage. While, for example, the Roman Catholic church discourages mixed marriages (though actually not too intensely) but will readily enough allow them if the "promises" are signed, Orthodox Judaism does not allow them at all. For a marriage to an "outsider" there are only two possibilities: that the Jew apostatize or that the outsider become religiously a Jew. The practices of Orthodox Judaism are so rigorous and —to a gentile—so esoteric, the likelihood of a genuine conversion in this direction is not great. Furthermore, Judaism not being a "missionary" religion, such an outcome is not expected. And there is another reason why this possibility is not too significant: among those of Jewish origin most likely to fall in love with Christians—those of the present generation who have broken out of the family circle either through their educational experience or through greater social breadth— Orthodox Judaism is very much on the decline.

Among Conservative and Reform Jews—and especially among the latter—there has been much greater assimilation into the general stream of American culture, and hence there is considerably more likelihood of the contacts which make the mixed marriage problem a likely possibility. But even here it is hard to generalize. The degree to which there is devotion to the "way of life," its dietary regulations, its feasts and fasts and the seriousness with which Jewish theology and literature are taken, varies from synagogue to synagogue and from family to family. Even here, however, there is official disapproval of mixed marriages (see page 79). However the likelihood that the non-Jew could conform to a particular measure of Jewish loyalty that his prospective mate represents is of course greater than in the case of Orthodox Judaism and the likelihood that the Jewish party will be open to consideration of Christian faith is also somewhat greater—though still considerably limited by factors yet to be discussed. Even in these more liberal Jewish groups family solidarity is greater than in the case of most Christian families. Hence it is not surprising that the largest number of mixed marriage cases arise in the case of Jews of the fourth group—those who, religiously speaking, are in fact secularists.

It would be difficult to say how large a proportion of younger Jews is in this group. Because those who regard themselves as so "emancipated" are the ones by far the most likely to be in social contact with others, especially in schools and colleges, one easily gains the impression that most young Jews are in this group. Whether this is true or not, as far as the particular problem we are considering, we may as well so conclude. How secularized a given Jew is is just as variable a matter as how secularized a particular gentile is. In both cases the naturalistic assumptions about life may be unconscious, the discorrelation with family belief and practice being a case of having "drifted away," or it may be a conscious and intentional rebellion against the family religion. As in the case of gentiles, the degree to which it is the latter is often in direct proportion to the rigor of that which has been abandoned. Just as the most intense secularists among those of Christian background are usually those who have thrown over a fundamentalist or Roman Catholic tradition, likewise, it would appear most intense secularists among Jews are those of Orthodox parentage or lineage. There are three characteristics of the Jewish "religious D.P." which should be noted—each of which has its parallels among lapsed Christians, especially those of the types mentioned:

1. There may be a nominal conformity on certain great days of the ecclesiastical year, either out of family feeling, or because these occasions have been rationalized into cultural holidays and folk festivals.

2. On the occurrence of the great moments in personal or family history (births, anniversaries, marriages, deaths), sentiment and family loyalty—and perhaps a measure of unrecognized nostalgia (the religious vacuum is never quite complete) may renew the old ties. Here sometimes feeling wins over thought (though it is to be noted that more often than not in the rebellion feeling won over thought).

3. Though the unbeliever may regard his position as "scientific" he usually indulges in the very unscientific attitude of overgeneralization: his distaste for his family religion usually expresses itself as a distaste for all religion, now matter how different other possibilities may be from that which he has rejected.

But the parallel breaks down somewhat as to the last factor. While general prejudice against the other group is probably higher among Christians than among Jews, religious prejudice against the other group is probably higher among Jews than among Christians. This is for a reason that is hardly to the credit of either Christianity or the gentile culture generally. The prejudice—and persecution—over the centuries has often expressed itself in the name of Christian belief and loyalty and hence it is not surprising that the Jew, either consciously or through a sort of "racial unconscious," translates his resentments as to these unfair attitudes and treatment to a resentment of Christianity as a religion. While the enlightened Christian today in thinking of the historic fact that "the Jews killed Christ" thinks only of particular Jewish leaders who, with the collaboration of the Roman authorities, saw to it that Jesus was crucified, Christians by and large over the centuries have not been so discriminating in their understanding of the situation and have thought of the Jews as the enemy of Christ. And in fact these thoughts have tended to become reality: this has made many Jews "the enemies of Christ."[1] Fortunately for future intercultural relations, all of this is on the wane and the greater understanding on the part of Christians—and repentance for a bad past in this regard—is in fact being matched by a much greater openness to respect for Jesus as a person and for Christian ethical teaching. But more often the very Jews who have thus overcome the group attitudes are ones

[1] As to the degree to which, generally unintentionally, these attitudes have been furthered by some Sunday School curricula, and conscientious steps have been taken in the preparation of other curricula in order to abate this tendency, see the chapter on "Roots of Bias" in my *Our Christmas Challenge* (published by Sterling Publishing Co., 1961).

who have also in their own minds "emancipated" themselves from the supernatural positions of their own heritage and thus are especially affronted by the supernatural claims of Christianity, since in the Incarnation and the New Testament accounts of the life, miracles and Resurrection of Christ the supernatural is even more vividly portrayed than in customary Judaism.

Further, whereas the secularist gentile—especially if he is liberal on social issues—may believe that religion has done more harm than good dividing people from each other, he has not felt the pressure and hurt of this division to the degree that the Jew has; hence if the latter is antireligious, he is likely to be so *ex animo* with more intensity than the gentiles.

This analysis is not made by way of condemnation but by way of understanding. In fact under the circumstances any other attitude would be surprising; and when another attitude exists (as it often does in individuals) it is in fact surprising. On the other hand, it would be surprising to find a gentile secularist who had any special animus against Judaism, since he has had no special reason to be offended by it religiously— or culturally, for that matter.

Now no secularist is really neutral as to religion. If religion be defined as the whole set of presuppositions which make up one's world view the secularist has a religion and the dogmas of that religion (articulated or assumed) differ from the dogmas of other religions just as dogmas of the Roman Catholic differ from those of the Lutheran, and those of the Orthodox Jew from those of the Mormon. And especially—for the reasons just indicated—the Jewish secularist is not neutral.

Case 30. Walter, of Jewish origin but an "unbeliever," and Cynthia, an agnostic of Unitarian background, arrange to have a quiet wedding in a college chapel. Walter asked the chaplain if the cross need be left on the altar during the service. Cynthia joins him in the request but simply out of regard for his feelings and not because the presence of the cross there would bother her personally. Yet as an intellectual matter, she—and her Unitarian parents—have no more belief in the Christian doctrine of the Atonement than Walter has.

It may seem a superficial point, but actually it is quite revealing. The same is true of the following illustration:

> *Case* 31. Louise, a Universalist, and Fred, a non-practicing Jew, are planning to be married by a Methodist minister. The Methodist marriage office contains an invocation of the Trinity ("in the Name of the Father and the Son and the Holy Spirit"). Though Louise disbelieves in the Trinity as thoroughly as does Fred she is not disposed to request the omission of the phrase; but he is so disposed.

Separable as the religious problem is in logic, in real life it is generally interwoven with the social problem; hence we will consider it briefly before proceeding to an analysis of solutions.

THE SOCIAL PROBLEM

There are those to whom the very mention of "problem" of this type implies prejudices or an endorsement of existent attitudes or strictures. Especially those in love will dismiss such considerations with a righteous fervor and in this they will be encouraged by those friends who have been brought up with the right social attitudes. But it is misleading in this field, as in others, to confuse *oughts* with *is's*. Whether these factors are to be regarded as barring marriage or not, they do exist as facts, like many other unwholesome group and individual attitudes. Therefore they should be recognized in their effects on the happiness of individual marriages and assessed so that any decision reached is a realistic one.

The operation of prejudice of this type is too widely known —and experienced—to labor the discussion. In a measure— and in its least vicious aspect—the barriers that exist are a particular application in this field of relations of the barriers and tensions that exist between any groups in society where there have been different orientations impinging upon the development of the individuals, whether cultural, economic, educational or a matter of family custom. There is no reason in ethics why a rich young man should not marry a poor girl— and indeed the Cinderella theme has been a very winsome one throughout the ages; but it is true that difficulties do arise (certainly not unsurmountable) in the mutual family adjustments and even in the personal adjustments of the parties. So too when a Ph.D. marries a young lady who has not finished high school. And granting parallel educational and economic backgrounds, matters of geography and past association play their part: a liaison between the debutante of an old Boston family and the son of a nouveau riche Texas oilman can suggest the picture. The fact is that customs, interests, reactions and the family background of a Jew—even a second- or third-generation one—are apt to be different from the environment out of which a gentile—churchgoing or not—has come. It is true that all these factors are leveling off in our time (though, it must be said, sometimes with an impoverishing loss of the distinctive virtues and tastes which arose from them).

But in the case of the Jewish-gentile relationship it must be admitted that the resulting barriers have a considerably less justifiable basis than other barriers of environment. Plain prejudice is there, and people still tend to associate with every representative of another group the characteristics and deeds of the least desirable members, while at the same time attributing to their own group the most desirable features which have ever expressed themselves therein. And the problem is not entirely just one of anti-Semitism. Jewish families harbor equal feelings toward the *goyim,* feeling a superiority—which is indeed sometimes the case, but which is often a group reaction to the inference of inferiority which various gentile discriminations have brought about. Because (more in the past than in the present) Jews have generally had inferior social, educational and professional opportunities, they are often suspicious of the motives of a Jew who is contemplating marriage to a gentile and especially if he is in fact open to the idea of working out his marriage in a Christian framework. Indeed if he is converted to Christianity his own group is inclined to doubt the sincerity of his decision and attribute it, at the worst, to "social climbing" and, at the best, to "compromise."

Among refined people a surface ease of relationship may have been indeed established with the respective parents and between them. Often however these relationships are worked out after a marriage has been viewed as inevitable, the prejudices and resentments continuing beneath the surface, and expressing themselves readily enough in manifold ways— especially if the marriage should enter rough times, even if the difficulties which arise in the marriage and in the family relationships may not be connected with this factor at all. And of course in many cases families stand resolute in their bias and continue to give the spouse and relatives of the other group a cold reception, if indeed they have not closed the door.

These feelings and tensions do not yield readily to logic, nor are they manageable by the reference back to previous liberal sentiments expressed by the parties involved.

> *Case* 32. Mrs. Teale as a trustee of her college had fought vigorously for the removal of all racial and religious barriers in the admission policy and had led the move for the elimination of restrictions in the college's social clubs. It was naturally a surprise to her daughter to find her mother nevertheless shocked when she announced her attachment to a Jewish student. But the mother still took refuge in generalities such as "I don't think it is wise," and "I don't think it would work out."

And parents often forget their own rebelliousness when it comes to the marriage of their children.

> *Case* 33. Mrs. Ronson had been bold indeed—especially in her day—to risk ostracism by her "set" in marrying a man

of no means and social standing from "the other side of the tracks"—and a Roman Catholic to boot. But she seemed not to recall this when discussing with her daughter the latter's contemplated marriage to a Jew.

People can sometimes forget their own background if a change has occurred in it.

Case 34. Dr. and Mrs. Stein, of Jewish origin, a few years before coming to this country had become Christians. They were respected members of a parish church in a medium-sized community. Although in no way did they seek to conceal their Jewish background they came to be a familiar part of the social and intellectual life of the city. When their daughter, also a Christian, announced her affection for a Jewish law student, they were opposed. They were ostensibly concerned on religious grounds, for indeed the Jew was a typical secularist. But when their minister who was counseling the couple told them that he thought there was a chance that the young man might become a Christian and he was reading some books that the minister had given him they were little comforted. (It is true that the boy's family environment had been typically "Jewish" and that the young lady's had not.)

Entirely apart from parents and relatives, the friends and business associates of the parties often became quite "cool" in their relationships, and the degree to which future ties can be made is somewhat impinged upon. Difficulties as far as clubs and resorts are concerned are well known enough. How important these less personal factors may be depends entirely upon the makeup, habits and priority scale of values of the two individuals. How important all of these factors, including personal relationships and family ruptures, are, curiously enough, is tied up with the religious question, even though these factors themselves have nothing directly to do with religion. How this is so we will now see.

THE SOLUTION

Just as in the analysis of the problem it is important to start with the religious question, so in the procedure for its solution that is where we should start. All the points in Chapter VII are relevant here. What the couples are religiously should be reassessed entirely apart from the faith of the parents or past attitudes taken by the parties themselves either in affirmation of that faith or in rebellion from it. The religious grounding of the marriage, and the religious sincerity on the part of each of the individuals, are more important factors than what parents will think, or whether sincerity will be attributed to any proposed changes or not.

Where the emphasis should lie in this religious quest will depend upon where the couple starts. If the Jew is serious about his religion (we can assume he is not Orthodox, but Conservative or Reform) and the Christian is serious about his, a mutual study of each position on a fifty-fifty basis is certainly appropriate. If, as is more often the case, the Christian has a more or less genuine connection with a religious tradition and the Jew has become secularized, even he may feel no particular interest in having the two of them undergo an exploration of Judaism; but in this case he should certainly give serious study to Christianity, both in the form in which his fiancée espouses it and in the form of other likely alternatives. Or both may be in fact secularists. In this case, as in any marriage, a rethinking of what the religious basis of the union is to be may lead to consideration of the possibilities of a mutually-held faith.

But in none of these situations should a result be reached as a compromise, either by one or by both. As has been suggested at length above, a person's religion is too important to be espoused *because* of a loved one, nor should one give up all or part of one's religious convictions in order to "split the difference" with the proposed spouse. Disloyalty to deepest convictions is a poor way to start any new human relationship.

If in fact change is called for on a basis of thoughtful convictions, then conversion by one of them to the faith of the other, or the mutual adoption of a halfway house is then desirable.

Case 35. William, a Presbyterian, and Martha, a Reform Jew, decided to become Unitarians. While in the realm of ethos and custom Martha has given up more, in the realm of doctrine she has given up nothing and William has given up a good deal. Whether or not this is a good idea depends entirely upon whether or not in all sincerity William came after careful study to disbelief in the Divinity of Christ. If he has, it is a quite proper solution; otherwise, it is not.

Nevertheless *how important are the other factors?* This question has been deferred until last because it cannot be answered until after the religious question has been answered. How important the other factors are depends principally upon what religious solution has been reached. If the couple has a positive and mutually-held religious faith as a basis of their new union the centripetal force it will represent should be sufficient to hold things together in spite of the centrifugal forces represented by family opposition and social restriction. Indeed if they have found a positive religious solution and are in love, it would be unworthy of them to rate these factors so high as to be a barrier to the marriage. On the other hand, if they had not found a positive religious solution to hold the marriage together, then these other factors will loom much larger in their destructive effect upon the peace and fruitfulness of their relationships. This is no vindication of the existence of these other factors in society; it is simply the recital of a fact.

Just "love" may not be enough to counteract what will be continuing sources of tension and frustration. But with a deep religious conviction, which affords the couple and the individual a transcendence over the particular environmental surroundings forced upon them and which offers a meaning for life beyond evil and tragedy, every blow, pressure or restriction from without can be an occasion of greater strength within. Indeed the virtues of this strength will become the goodly heritage of their children.

❧❧

CHAPTER IX

"WE'RE BOTH PROTESTANTS"

IT WOULD SEEM, from all that has gone before, that if neither of the two prospective mates is Roman Catholic or Jewish no religious problems imperil them. This apparently happy situation is usually announced in terms of our chapter heading: "We're both Protestants."

But the situation is not that simple, for two reasons:

There are many kinds of non-Roman Christians—differing in significant particulars.

The word "Protestant" not only covers the churches which reflect Reformation theology; it also means "miscellaneous"—and is used for such diverse possibilities as Mormons, Christian Scientists, Ethical Culturists, and outright secularists affiliated with nothing.

There are important ways in which a high-church Presbyterian is nearer in basic belief to a Roman Catholic than to a Unitarian. Actually high-church Episcopalians—and, interestingly enough, many Baptists—do not regard themselves as Protestants at all.

There are two reasons for the common—and convenient—overgeneralization here, both reasons being the same at root:

People forget the *positive* role of religion in a marriage (a matter already covered).

People tend to conceive of the problem of mixed marriages in terms of barriers and arrangements as to *getting* married rather than as a problem of the marriage itself.

These misconceptions are encouraged by the fact that in the case of two "Protestants" the arrangements are in fact so simple. There is recognition of the validity of the marriage all round, and there are no threats of excommunication (except in the case of a few obscure sects). All too often no marriage counseling[1] is provided before the service and hence any religious problems which may be implicit in the situation are not unearthed and aired.

On the other hand, in those families and communities where such interdenominational marriages would be questioned it is often family loyalty or even prejudice that comes to the fore rather than a constructive concern for the religious unity of the new family and encouragement of mutual truth-seeking.

The mention of these latter concepts will remind the reader that, just as in the case of the last chapter, there is nothing new in principle involved here. In fact, a good many examples from this field have already been used as illustrations in the general discussion of mixed marriages. Of necessity then the material in this chapter will be in part repetitious. But since readers of a book cannot be counted on to read it entirely or to go beyond a chapter which seems to cover their immediate concern, all that bears on this problem will be at least summarized here, with reference back to the fuller discussion of each point. On the other hand, we will here give fuller discussion to certain special points which were mentioned only in passing in the earlier pages of this book.

[1] Such counseling is required by the canon law of the Episcopal Church [Canon 17, § 2(d)] and is increasingly being provided by many ministers of other churches.

COMMON GROUND

First, we should recognize the truth that lies behind the easy assumption that if both parties are Protestant all is well. No matter how great the differences between groups so classified, there is a great deal by way of belief, attitude and custom that is held in common, and many of these are factors which have significant unitive function in the marriage. Among these are the following:

1. The primacy of a direct relationship to God or to principles in the realm of conscience.

2. The conviction that celibacy is not a higher vocation than marriage.

3. A responsible role for the layman in the institutional life of the Church.

4. An emphasis (except for the secularists) upon the Bible and on the intuitions which come to the individual from reading the same.

5. A recognition (on the part of all but a few) that no one group can claim to be the *true* Church and "unchurch" all the rest.

6. The acceptance of what Paul Tillich has called "the Protestant principle": that all institutions are under judgment and *need* reformation (the trait of self-criticism applied to the group).

7. A common heritage (for most) of hymnody and devotional material, and worship in the vernacular.

8. A belief in religious liberty—including freedom to evangelize—for all other groups.

The bearing of these notions on a marriage in its internal and external relationships are too obvious to require comment. Equally obvious is the divisive effect of the holding of opposite attitudes by one of the two parties. For elaboration of these points and for discussion of others applicable to a narrower grouping (more or less "main-line" reformed Churches) the books listed in the bibliography under "Protestant (in general)" (page 98) should be consulted.

POINTS OF TENSION

To state the other side of the picture, it would logically be necessary to analyze all non-Roman groups point by point. But as to specific differences—important or trivial—between any two given traditions, we shall have to refer the reader to the bibliography (page 96) or to clergy representing the specific churches. However, to help those who do make such further exploration discern the more significant differences which may have a bearing on a marriage we will here outline certain major cleavages.

1. *Fundamentalism vs. modernism.* The person who "sits loose" to the details of Scripture naturally assumes that the many differences of Biblical interpretation do not matter. But the fundamentalist does not view it that way. The literal acceptance of narrative, prophecy and prescription is thought of as fundamental to being a Christian. And this barrier is not of one-sided construction: a wall is also erected by the modernist's sense of intellectual superiority and even contempt for literalist views.

2. *"Liberalism" vs. "orthodoxy."* This distinction has to do with individual reaction to the classical doctrines of Christianity. While the liberal is apt to say "doctrines don't matter," the more conservative churchman thinks they do and may even discern that the liberal has his own dogmas, that is, convictions about what is most important in the world. The "inevitable progress of man" unaided by God is as much a dogma as the doctrine of original sin, and each colors one's view of human possibilities and of the means of fulfillment. Here again each party is likely to feel superior in his "emancipation" or "faithfulness."

3. *"Open" vs. "closed" membership.* Since a sense of equality of status is important in a marriage, the way a party is

treated in the other's Church is important. There is a variety
of practice here. Most Churches will not accept persons not
baptized in the name of the Trinity; a number will not recognize those not baptized by immersion; some even decline to
recognize immersion by some other group than their own.

There is a cleavage between those groups which will admit
to the Holy Communion all Christians and those which admit
only members of the particular Church or congregation. And
as to membership, while most will accept a "letter of transfer"
from another denomination, others require a new profession
of faith or confirmation.

Sometimes behind these rules lie attitudes of actual hostility
toward other Churches; sometimes not.

4. *Forms of worship.* The very mention of the word "form"
would seem to imply the unimportance of distinctions. But
actually the principal relationship of most people to their
Churches is the experience of worship. Here especially much
more than the mind is involved, and responses are often un-
susceptible of critical analysis. When a Baptist says of Lutheran worship, "I just don't feel at home in that church," or
the Lutheran says of a prayer meeting, "I don't feel I have
been to church," there is more—and less—involved than mental note-taking and point-by-point comparison.

Further confusion is engendered by the fact that those accustomed to "free" worship verbalize their distaste for litur-
gical worship by eschewing all "form and ceremony," rarely
recognizing that they too have their forms and ceremonies.
An academic gown is no less a form than a surplice, and
"free" prayer has its pattern. Quietness in church (of either
the Quaker or the Episcopalian) is a form; talk and customary
greetings in church are a form. Words are forms; gestures are
forms. Again these feelings of superiority and scorn; they
appear in the edge to such comments as "We don't need those
'props' to prayer"; "We stand in the *great* tradition of worship."

The most important difference here is in the place of the
Holy Communion or the Lord's Supper in the devotional life

of the individual. With groups as otherwise different as the Disciples of Christ and the Episcopal Church it is a weekly opportunity; with most other groups it is an infrequent mode of worship. And to few Christians is it a matter of mere form, no matter which tradition one espouses.

5. *Ethics.* Owing to a combination of Puritan and pietistic influences in the development of American religion many Protestant denominations are still officially convinced of the sinfulness of drinking, smoking, dancing, etc. And the attitude of other groups to the contrary is not viewed as a variant ethical attitude: it is stamped as "looseness"—a lower morality. And the negativistic attitude toward sex held by many groups has a definite bearing on marital adjustment.[2]

Also there are non-Roman Christians who take a view toward contraception not unlike that of the Roman Catholic Church (see Chapter III).

FACTORS FAVORABLE TO A SOLUTION

Candor as to possible difficulties is not meant to suggest a "no" answer to marriage, any more than in the main discussion in earlier chapters. It is simply meant as an alert to the problem and a focus for the solution. And, as a matter of fact, in marriages in the general area we are now considering there are a number of factors which make a sound solution more likely.

First of all, the use in our society of the general appellation "Protestant," undiscriminating as it may be, serves to relieve the social barriers and ease the prejudices which enter into reactions of relatives and friends. While, as we have seen, there may be very real problems, the fact that people are less likely to *think* of it as a problem is in itself a help. Second, the fact that the Churches which might reasonably provide the forum for the marriage will not be requiring an undertaking as to the religious upbringing of the children leaves that an open matter to be decided by the couple—and not

[2] On these various points see the chapter on "Inhibition" in the author's *Beyond Anxiety* (Scribner's, 1953).

necessarily at the time of the marriage. Third, the validity or religious nature of the marriage will be in question by neither party or his relatives, since there is a general recognition of other bodies as parts of the Christian Church and as having capacity to marry all those who in good faith resort to them. Fourth, there is no barrier—in terms of "sin"—to mutual participation in the worship of either party's church, or of any other which may be under scrutiny. Finally, the decision to be made will not be the black-and-white one of which is *the true Church,* but which is the *truest,* that is, which holds greatest measure of truth on the important questions; not which is the *good* Church, but which is the *best,* that is, offers the fullest nourishment for the spiritual life of its adherents.

But it is these very favorable factors which tend to hide the fact that there is a significant problem nevertheless. The outline of religious differences was provided to counteract this tendency. The same is the purpose of this summary of possibilities.

WHAT CAN HAPPEN

If the religious differences are left unresolved one of the following may be the outcome:

1. Uprooted by their diversity and probably by a new locale, the couple may stop attending church altogether, or drift from church to church, becoming what are called "ecclesiastical tramps." If this is as a result of careful conscious decision—that's one thing; if it's by default, it's another.

2. The couple may attend the church of the more aggressive partner. This may reflect a real change of conviction on the part of the other party; but, if not, it may serve simply as a conspicuous external expression of what may already be an unfortunate domination of one personality by another, with perhaps an intensification of unconscious resentments.

3. The couple may attend the nearest church of either denomination, or perhaps just the nearest church. Whatever may be said for this by way of convenience, it represents a

superficial handling of the problem of real denominational differences—unless it so happens that the denomination of the nearest church happens to represent the thought-through convictions of the couple. And because of the high mobility of population these days this problem is apt to repeat itself, disturbing the continuity of loyalty of the children to a religious tradition—which is important at all times in life, but especially in formative years.

4. The couple may decide to go to a "community church" which may call itself "nondenominational" or "interdenominational." This may seem to avoid a choice; but actually it is the choice of a third denomination; since this given church has *some* position which characterizes its teachings from the pulpit and in its Sunday school classrooms.

Case 36. John is a Presbyterian, Mary a Methodist, both having never questioned the Divinity of Christ. They decide to resolve the difference by affiliating with the local Community Church, whose minister and director of religious education are Unitarians. Now if by thoughtful conviction John and Mary have decided that the Divinity of Christ is either not so or is unimportant, then they have made a permissible decision; but it is not right to abandon so important a belief *by default*.

THE SOLUTION

This illustration leads directly to the solution.

If the parties belong to Churches it is likely that they are what they are because of birth or some accidental factor in their youth. As we have said before, the fact that one's parents are in a particular tradition does not mean it is the best or truest. If one or both have no church connection that too may be accidental—or the result of a youthful rebellion or drift, without careful mature study of the case for various religious alternatives.

Therefore what is called for is an open-minded examination

—together—of the positions and claims of the two alternative traditions represented by the couple, or of any other likely possibilities. This should include attendance at the respective churches, consultation with clergy and others familiar with the traditions involved, reading of representative literature. All this has been discussed more fully in Chapter VII.

But as we have already seen, there is a less crucial issue involved than when there is a Roman Catholic party—not because of the unimportance of certain differences but because this process of exploration can go on before or after marriage without a decision being required in order to make arrangements for the marriage itself and because there are no canonical, and fewer psychological, barriers to free exploration.

But the unity of family life and a dependable religious matrix for the children nonetheless depend upon a mature and mutually satisfactory decision. And if time will permit, the work preparatory to decision should be done before marriage and the decision sealed by the marriage ceremony itself, conducted in the tradition which will be counted on to be the channel of meaning and the means of grace over the years.

CHAPTER X

FOR THOSE ALREADY IN
A MIXED MARRIAGE

THE DETAILED ANALYSIS furnished by the earlier chapters of
this book with respect to the difficulties involved in mixed
marriages does not imply any judgment toward those who are
in fact already so married. Nor is there any implication that
every such marriage must necessarily be a failure or that one
cannot point to certain mixed marriages which appear to be
more successful than marriages of persons of the same religious faith. We have simply tried to be realistic about the
factors which enter into a mixed marriage and to be honest
about the relatively unsatisfactory character of such marriages
in general terms, as is reflected by the statistics on them. Least
of all do we imply that those already involved in mixed marriages should separate. Naturally, in spite of whatever degree
the difference in religious orientation infringes upon the complete happiness of the marriage, the best should be made of
it. This chapter is concerned with the ways and means toward
this best.

We will turn first to the relations between the couples
themselves and second to the problems connected with the
religious upbringing of the children.

SILENCE OR SHARING?

It is a common notion that the best way to keep peace on the religious frontier is for the subject to be avoided. If in fact the professed religion of either or both of the parties is uninteresting to the party holding it, then it is probably time that he sought a new religious faith that will have meaning for him. But if in fact one's faith is part of one's life, silence about it is impossible without unfortunate effects upon the personality and upon interpersonal relations. More than that, a person has a duty to talk about—and present attractively—his religious convictions. If a man believes something to be the truth, naturally he should feel it his duty to make it known to those around him, especially those closest to him. This duty is reinforced by one of the promises which the Roman Catholic party in a mixed marriage must make; namely the promise to seek to make a Roman Catholic out of the non-Roman party. While the non-Roman party has signed a promise not to seek to influence the Roman party to his faith, nevertheless he is under a general obligation to seek to persuade all men to what he regards to be the truth. Thus his promise is again the forswearing of an obligation (as in the case of the religious upbringing of the children discussed above) and thus is not binding, since a person cannot promise not to do what are his duties; he can only give away his *rights*. But would not the fulfilling of this obligation on the part of the non-Roman party and of this obligation on the part of the Roman party bring turmoil into the marriage?

Not necessarily. If the spouses face the subject frankly together and agree to talk interestedly and listen sympathetically as to the religious convictions each holds, creative influences could be let loose in the marriage which would mitigate in some measure the basic defect involved in a mixed marriage. Any good thing like this can come into a marriage only at a risk, but it is a risk worth taking—if the parties undertake it mutually.

A GUIDE TO INTERFAITH SHARING

This approach to bringing religion "out in the open" should follow some rules like the following:

1. Don't let your partner feel that he or she is talking to a blank wall. Focus with interest on what is being said.

2. Take the initiative in bringing up the subject of the beliefs, practices and activities of your partner's church. Opening the subject "out of the blue" is much more reassuring than attention granted after the subject is opened.

3. Limit questions with a critical tinge to specific subject matters and "pad" them well with agreement or understanding as to other realms of the same subject.

4. Stress common ground; seek to translate concepts and practices into the other person's religious terminology so that agreement on substance can be made evident—where such is honestly the case.

5. Ground whatever differences can be honestly so grounded in differences in historical orientation and surrounding mores; and make a careful distinction between essentials and nonessentials.

6. "Lay off" certain points which have shown themselves to be creative of tension and misunderstandings; do not keep going over and over the same ground.

7. Stress the positive resources of faith and joy which have significant bearing on the couple's daily lives. Actually put the theological and ethical insights of your tradition to work, in the discussion of family problems and decisions about future plans. This is the best way to commend them.

8. If your religious worship and interest bring you joy and excite your enthusiasm (and if they do not then you had better find another Church yourself), let this show itself; and it will be hard for even the most rigorous separatist and "exclusivist" in religion not to concede that "there are diversities of gifts, but the same Spirit. And there are differences of administrations, but the same Lord. And there are diversi-

ties of operations, but it is the same God which worketh all in all." (I Corinthians 12:4–6)

9. In your reaction to your spouse's religious interest and motivation, recognize inwardly, as well as in words—whatever may be your disagreement with certain theological points— that nevertheless it is the same God as the One you worship Who is the center of your spouse's concern. (This, of course, assumes that you both believe in God. Even if you don't both believe in God or in Christ, concede all possible ground in the field of religion and/or ethics—and do so ungrudgingly.)

10. Take the trouble to learn all you can about your partner's faith, its history, its doctrines and its characteristic attitudes, as well as the meaning of its forms and ceremonies. Ignorance is often misconstrued as bigotry—and often it is, because it reflects an unwillingness to have found out what the facts are.

11. Separate issues of belief from personalities. If a reliable pattern along this line has been established in the home, then no repercussions will follow because the non-Roman party does not like a particular Roman Catholic priest or because the Roman Catholic party is irritated by a particular non-Roman priest or minister—and for that matter a person in whose church the unsatisfactory parson ministers can thus be free to express, without embarrassment or fear that a point will be made of it, his own dissatisfaction with the incumbent.

12. Make a point of having grace at meals and family prayers. Those whose religion does not allow them to say "Amen" to the prayers of other religionists should simply refrain from saying it; but there is no law in any church against a respectful silence. The prayer reaches God anyway, with or without the "Amen," and the favorable effect upon family unity is not thereby completely canceled.

13. Whatever faith the children are being brought up in, see to it that they gain as favorable an impression as possible of the faith of the other party, that they see the points in common, that they know which differences are nonessential and

which are essential. And encourage them to respect the sincerity of the different religious allegiances.

14. If it is at all possible, have the entire family from time to time participate in the religion of the spouse who is in the minority.

WHAT RELIGION FOR THE CHILDREN?

Those whose marriage involves a Roman Catholic party to whose Church the children have been signed away may be tempted to omit this section. But actually they should not, because the question is not as settled as they may think. Of course, one has an obligation to fulfill one's contracts if the contracts are valid. But if a contract is void *ab initio*—that is, from the beginning—then there is no obligation to abide by it. Now in fact a contract that the children will be raised in another religious tradition than one's own is void *ab initio*—from an ethical point of view. Here is the reason (to review):

Every parent has a primary obligation to his children to bring to them the best spiritual orientation that he possibly can. This is not an obligation which he can delegate to others —though others may have to exercise it for him in particular periods of time and under particular circumstances. Being an obligation, it cannot be contracted away; only rights can be contracted away.

To repeat an earlier example, suppose a parent should make a contract with a research agency to feed his child nothing but starch for five years in order to see what effect it would have on his bodily development. Obviously such a contract would be void *ab initio*—both ethically and legally—because a parent has a primary responsibility to provide the best physical nurture he can for his child. Now if a non-Roman parent *really* believes that the Roman Catholic faith is the best spiritual nurture for his child, that is, that it represents the best and fullest truth, then he should himself become a Roman Catholic—and we would no longer have a mixed marriage to worry about. But if, for example, a Lutheran really believes the teachings of his church are nearer the truth than the teachings of the Roman Catholic Church and that the implications for living in this tradition are sounder than those in the Roman teaching, then he cannot validly contract to provide his child with what, for him, is second-rate religious fare, a diet that by his own standards involves spiritual "vitamin deficiencies."

The position that the antenuptial agreement as to the raising of children is not binding means that the question is always an open one. The question can never be dismissed from the conscience of either party. What if one of the partners is agnostic? Could he not reasonably settle his conscience by saying that since he doesn't know what he believes he should allow the child to be raised a Biblical fundamentalist or a Roman Catholic, since his spouse believes firmly in one or the other? I think we know what the answer would be if we asked the agnostic to give an honest answer to these questions: Do you really believe that the best liberating influences will come into the life of a child raised with a thoroughgoing fundamentalist or Roman Catholic indoctrination? If you really believe the teachings of the Bible taken literally or of Papal promulgation to be false, or at least unworthy of an intelligent man's conviction, can you really want your child to be grounding his attitudes and hopes in these very things? If you think the more "earth-bounded" attitudes you yourself espouse—either consciously or unconsciously, either in theory or in practice—are more intelligent and "realistic," should you not want your child to be so nurtured?

Now in saying that this matter is still on the conscience, I do not mean to imply that the partner who has committed his children to a tradition other than his own must necessarily seek to reverse that decision. But I do mean to say that if he decides to abide by it he does not do so because he has made a contract, but because abiding by it is the lesser of two evils as contrasted with the possible disruption of the marriage which might come from his reversing field. In other words, a decision to let things ride can quite properly be based on a present evaluation of the factors involved in this decision (including the effect on the marriage of "reversing field" when the other party has "acted in reliance"), rather than upon a sense of obligation about his previous promise—for there is no obligation as to that. But if he can find a time in the married life when he can reverse field and thus satisfy his own conscience, he should take advantage of it.

Case 37. Walter, a devout Episcopalian, and June, a devout Roman Catholic, have a child six years old. Walter has every reason to believe that his wife's love for him is greater than her allegiance to her church (as serious as this may be). It would not be wrong for him now to unburden to her his conscientious difficulty about the child being raised other than an Episcopalian, and fully recognizing the Roman Catholic baptism as satisfactory, express the desire to send him to an Episcopal school. In insisting on the point, however, he takes a calculated risk, namely, will this seriously threaten a disruption of the marriage—which disruption would normally be a greater evil than a father's nonfulfillment of his positive obligation toward the religious training of his children. Having weighed the risks, should he decide to press the matter of schooling he may seem to be taking advantage of his wife's weakness, but, on the other hand, in terms of his convictions, to do otherwise would be to take advantage of the child's weakness in this situation. In any case, it is the choice of the lesser of two evils and to be made after much prayerful searching of conscience.

Case 38. Wilhelmina is a staunch Roman Catholic, and does desire a good education for her child. Her husband, William, is a loyal Lutheran but, under the duress created by his strong love for Wilhelmina, he had signed the promises as to the raising of the children. The Roman Catholic parochial school in the neighborhood in which they live is extremely inadequate both in terms of equipment and educational standards. The Lutheran parochial school is one of the best schools in the state. William should take advantage of this "break" and seek to persuade Wilhelmina to change the educational orientation of their child.

Case 39. Marie, a Roman Catholic, under the influence of Rodney, a strong-minded Methodist, was married by a Methodist minister, because of Rodney's unwillingness to sign the promises. Now excommunicated, she feels religiously bereft. She is entitled to—and bound in duty—to express her distress to her husband and seek to persuade him to yield a point as to the raising of the children, so that they can be remarried by a Roman Catholic priest and she can return to the sacraments. But this action is not justified on the basis of parental pressure, but only on the assumption that she really believes the Roman Catholic faith, including the teaching that she is threatened with, namely, that without this readjustment of the situation she risks the loss of her soul forever.

RETHINKING RELIGIOUS ALLEGIANCES

But when all is said and done there is of course much left to be desired in any mixed marriage. However helpful the above suggestions and guides may be in a given marriage they are but makeshifts designed to "shore up" the situation. In the long run the best single thing a marriage can possess is a common religious grounding, just as the best thing an individual person can possess is a sound religious orientation.

Now we should never assume that this is a closed question, any more than we can assume that the religious nurture of the children can ever be a closed question. Adults in various conditions of life often take thought and change their religious ties. Especially should they *consider* doing so when they are in daily contact with a person for whom another alternative is obviously significant. Even more especially should they consider such a possibility if a living, working religious faith of a spouse stands in vivid contrast to their own lack of one. "I could never take all that supernatural business" or "I could never be a Catholic" or "Once a Catholic always a Catholic" —are all belied by the statistics on conversions in all directions.

An initial openness to the position of a spouse followed by a firmer adherence to one's own heritage is quite understandable. Such a result may simply mean that the more a spouse learned of the other religion, the less he found it—in his opinion—a possible choice for him! But all too often there is not such an opinion, and indeed the fact that a spouse holds a particular faith sometimes becomes the principal reason for not holding it. Sometimes something deeper is involved:

Case 40. Matilda "wears the pants" in the Williams family: she makes the decisions, runs the finances, does most of the talking. But Algernon Williams has one refuge: Matilda is a pillar of the Bible Christian Church and Algernon sits home and conspicuously regards the Bible as a blind guide. When he gets a chance to talk he quotes from George Bernard Shaw, Bertrand Russell, John Dewey, and Will Durant. Their "line" serves as an articulate symbol of his inarticulate resentment of his wife's domination.

Case 41. Alex is 100 per cent extrovert. His organizing and "sales" ability has projected him into leadership, not only in his business, but in his church. Nina is a quiet, shy soul. Though she was nominally connected with a church not so different from her husband's as to separate them, she declines to go to any church and interests herself in the writings of Aldous Huxley and Gerald Heard. In part this "mystical" emphasis reflects her own introversion; in part it is a symbol of her resentment of her husband's greater outgoingness—and on a front broader than the question of religion as usually conceived.

In one sense a problem so analyzed is not a "religious" one. But in another sense it is: the deep cleavages thus revealed can only be healed by an overarching religious influence. So, while in a superficial sense religion is the problem, in a more profound sense it is the answer—the answer to the healing of the marriage.

But where there are no special resentments to be expressed, no particular axes to grind, a party should be *more* attracted to his spouse's religion because his spouse holds it. As to the *way* to give serious consideration to another religious possibility, it is sufficient to refer back to Chapter VII, where this subject is discussed with reference to couples not yet married.

WHEN BOTH PARTIES STAND PAT

But even with an optimum of openness—and perhaps even eagerness—to find common grounds many couples will still find that they must in conscience differ religiously. If serious study and careful thought have in fact been given to the two alternatives—and to other plausible meeting grounds—then the matter need not be constantly reopened. One can rightly hope that during the open period came at least a better understanding and a deeper appreciation of each other's faith. What more is there to be said? One thing: the poorest way to commend one's "difference" from one's spouse is to fail to illustrate in practice the faith one has vigorously defended in discussion.

Case 42. Charles, raised a Disciple, is quite sure that it is better to be a Protestant than to be a Roman Catholic. Patricia, his Roman Catholic wife, has not had on tap very impressive arguments against his position. But Charles goes to church when he "feels like it," while Patricia goes every Sunday. It would appear that Patricia has won the argument.

CHAPTER XI

HELPING OTHERS IN
MIXED MARRIAGE SITUATIONS

INCREASINGLY people are confronted with other people's mixed marriage problems. This is not merely because of the increase in the number of such situations. It is also because the problem is of the sort that naturally suggests the idea of the use of an "outsider" for advice. One's priest, minister or rabbi is an obvious possibility. And college chaplains, school guidance officers, class advisers and the like are frequently called upon. But nonprofessionals too are often resorted to: a relative or friend, or a trusted acquaintance.

Of course, the primary requisite of any counselor in such a matter is that he understand the nature of the problem and that he has thought through the implications of various possible decisions. Hence, all that appears in the preceding pages bears on the fulfillment of the counselor's task and may be helpful to him. But there are several things that are peculiar to the role of one who is called upon to help others in these matters and hence in this chapter we will analyze the situation from that perspective.

There are two distinct roles for the counselor to play when a person or couple has come to him regarding a mixed mar-

riage, and much of the ineffectiveness of counsel in this regard is due to a failure to distinguish between these two roles.

The separate functions of the two roles are:

1. Impartial analysis of the problem, of the issues at stake,
and of the consequence of particular solutions.

2. Representation of the claims of one of the alternative religious traditions in the picture.

Speaking generally, the first role is an impartial one, the
second a partial one; in the first the role is that of *referee,* in
the second it is that of *advocate.*

Not every type of counselor will engage in the second function, but all should exercise the first. For example, it is not
part of the function of a public school guidance officer or college dean of women to parade before the counselee the merits
of a particular religious tradition, though it is both proper and
right that such a counselor help the counselee grasp what the
religious "mixture" implies for the marriage and family-to-be.
In this case he will enter upon the second function only to the
extent of referral. But a minister, for example, will quite properly move into this second phase at the right time. Yet it is
important that he has played the first role with care and candor until the couple fully understand their problem, before he
assumes the role of advocate. Hence we will discuss the two
tasks separately.

THE ROLE OF REFEREE

Much that is applicable here simply has to do with good
counseling techniques in any field, and may seem obvious to
the trained or experienced adviser. But they may not be so
obvious to the non-professional called upon for help, and in
any case certain attitudes and approaches—though generally
applicable—are of such special importance in this field, and
are in fact so often neglected, to the hurt of the situation, that
I am taking the risk of laboring the obvious in summarizing
them with particular reference to mixed marriage counseling.

Nothing could be more crucial to the outcome of a particular case than the spirit with which the couple is met. If confidence is inspired in the counselor in the role of referee that same confidence will carry over as he assumes the role of advocate. And even if he does not proceed to that role, the degree to which the couple will be open to a comparative approach to religious allegiance will depend in large measure upon the degree to which they respect the fairness of the counselor and his sensitiveness to their problem.

To the counselor, especially one who runs into this type of situation fairly often, the problem may appear to fall into a generalized category. Indeed reading a book like this may have encouraged such a response. But we must remember that to the couple theirs is a unique and non-recurring situation, of central importance to their lives. One's secretary may say, "Your next appointment is another mixed marriage situation," but this is not the way the couple would define it. To take an analogy from the clothing business, the fitting must be tailor-made and not ready-made.

To get on a particular basis immediately, after the usual small talk, the counselor should ask as to the religious background of each, and in so doing, should press beyond labels to discern the actual firmness of the allegiance, and whether it is based on "dogged loyalty," inertia, or actual mature conviction and regular practice.

Case 43. Alfred is a Roman Catholic, Dorothea is a Methodist.

Q. Alfred, how regularly do you go to Mass?

A. Well, not very often in the last three or four years. I go when I'm home on visits, and of course on Easter and Christmas.

Q. Dorothea, how about your church-going?

A. I go every Sunday morning, and generally to the evening service in connection with the meeting of the young adult group.

Q. Have you always been this active?

A. No, my interest developed when I was in college. I thought I didn't believe in much of anything; but a course in religion and some conferences with the chaplain straightened me out, and I've been reading a good deal on the subject ever since.

Q. Alfred, have you given much thought to your convictions in recent years? Done any reading?

A. No, not much. I've always been a Catholic and couldn't be anything else; but frankly my interests have generally not run to religion very much.

Now this is no time in the conference for drawing conclusions or giving a homily on the importance of religious concern. But the answers given bear on the subsequent direction of the conversation. And they set the stage for dealing with flesh-and-blood individuals, not textbook illustrations. Obviously they point to a genuine need of at least one of the parties—a need which transcends even the marriage problem—the need of religious maturity, indeed of conversion: to *what* being an open-end matter at this point.

This leads to the next factor in the counselor's approach: while he may want his Church or viewpoint to "win," it is most important at this phase of things that completely to the fore is concern for the individuals and the health of their prospective alliance. This is why they have come and they must be met in these terms. When the solution has finally been proposed, at the referee part of the counseling session, it is important that the counselor emphasize his sincerity in proposing mutual study and rethinking. It would be well to go so far as to say (this is easy for a lay counselor, difficult for a parson): "And if your study and thought lead you to become [whatever is other than the minister's church] and you decide on higher grounds that one's yielding to the other, then you will have a sounder marriage than if you remain religiously separated." I have been fortunate enough to have at hand for illustrative use at this point a true case which even further emphasizes the openness being recommended:

> *Case 44.* Peter, a Roman Catholic, and Cynthia, an Episcopalian, agreed to the mutual study plan, and really followed through. Peter decided to become an Episcopalian and Cynthia decided to become a Roman Catholic. The strength and the genuineness of their new-found convictions were such that both saw that the marriage would not be a good idea; but their regret over that was tempered in a measure by the fact that both saw in the situation "a means of grace," since both had been routine in their religion before and now both had the devotion of converts.

(Those who believe that love is more important in life than religion will wince at this one; but they can receive comfort from the fact that each is now happily married—to a person of his own faith.)

There is in most of these situations a special reason why the counselor should lean over backward in openness as to the answers the parties may reach. Usually one or both are being subjected to pressures from parents and other relatives, and perhaps from the family priest or minister, who talk little of independent decision on the merits and much of "loyalty," "apostasy," "superstition," "giving up your religion," and often with all the emotional stops pulled out: "It will kill your father!" "We won't be able to face our friends." "We've always been . . ." etc. One can sympathize—and should in the conference—with these quite natural family reactions, but it is important that there be at least one person in the picture who treats the parties as adults, respecting their integrity, and trusting them to make honest inquiry and attempt sincere decisions.

As soon as the matter of family pressures comes out in the discussion (and the counselor should ask questions to bring it forth) the counselor should set them in the proper priority scale. It's not that they should be ignored, but that they should be faced as a secondary question after the main question has been faced and answered. Assure them of your interest in advising them, at the proper time, as to how best to deal with parents and others once the main decision is made, and also remind them of what wide experience has shown: parents are not generally as intractable after the event as they threaten to be beforehand—especially if the couple maintain from their side a sympathetic and loving attitude (and effort) toward the aggrieved ones. Later in the chapter we will consider ways to ameliorate this aspect of the situation. But at this point it should be made clear that whatever the outcome with parents, the first concern is the soundest possible basis for *this marriage*. If that is not achieved outside pressures do become of primary importance; if it is, they can be managed—even a closed door to one's home, or being "cut off without a dime."

To conclude this first phase of the counselor's relationship with the couple a book like this one may well be provided for them. If the timing permits it might be better for them to read it before the discussions are resumed and the advocacy stage entered. It might seem to be a shortcut to give them such a book and then move directly to the second role, but even as the author of this particular effort I could not urge too strongly against such a procedure. *The personal approach to the particular problem is primary,* and unless the couple is flatly unwilling to come and talk, a book should never take the place of the personal attention to their particular problem with which the whole relationship should begin—and end (if indeed it does end).

THE TRANSITION BETWEEN THE TWO ROLES

As to the next step, the situation differs as to whether or not the counselor is himself a representative of one of the religious allegiances involved. In either case referral is involved, and the usual bases of sound referrals apply; but again it is well to review the situation with particular reference to the type of problem we are considering.

The non-clergy counselor. If the couple is set adrift at this point, there is always danger that they will not "carry through" but will allow an unconscious fear that a mutual decision will not be reached to encourage dilatoriness about the reading and counsel they have agreed to undertake. The result may be a snap decision or "the line of least resistance"—which may or may not correspond to the decision they would have made had they taken the harder course. Therefore it is important that the counselor lead them to the next steps. As to reading, definite titles should be furnished them (selected from the bibliography in Chapter VII, or otherwise in the counselor's mind or files). As to instruction from clergy, it is advisable to make recommendations to supplement the individuals' contacts. Often, especially if both are "regular" in their religious practices, it is enough to have it agreed that both will go to each other's priest, minister or rabbi. But sometimes one or both are out of touch with the Church, or lack confidence in a particular incumbent—either in general or for this particular type of task (the type that evokes these familiar comments: "Dr. Weatherby is a wonderful man, but I can't see him being of much help in this situation," or "Father Williams is a good priest, but I think his manner would put John off"). Here is where at least the professional counselor should be equipped with names of local clergy of the principal traditions in whom he has confidence and who he feels will represent the given positions at their best and will be likely to handle conferences in this field with intelligence and sympathy. Such a list is developed through experience on the job and a "carry through" on particular cases which enables the counselor to profit through the process of trial-and-error. Relationships with clergy suitable for such referrals can be strengthened—and the counseling transition eased—if the non-clergy counselor will call the clergy involved, state that the referral is being made, and "brief" them on the case, expressing willingness to be of further help (in the referee role) at any further point.

The clergy counselor. All that is said above applies here

too, except that there will normally be one less referral: presumably he will be one of the spokesmen functioning in the second phase of the matter. But he should be just as concerned that an adequate person represent the other side, and especially if the couple is at a loss in this regard he should know his community and its available clergy well enough to be able to make sound suggestions. He should also be humble enough to suggest another spokesman for his own tradition, if he really believes another considerably more adequate than himself; but the superiority should be marked, because normally the couple will feel more secure if at least one factor in the arrangement remains constant. And, as a matter of fact, he—and his tradition—have an initial advantage in the situation if he has discharged his first role helpfully.

As to whether he will want to get in touch with his recommendee for the other side will depend on his knowledge of the Churches and personalities involved. Where feelings are high, and especially where the other Church does not favor reciprocal re-examination of religious allegiances, silence may be the best policy. But where feasible, such open dealing on the whole matter cannot but help further ecumenical relations in the community as well as sweeten the atmosphere for the given counselees.

THE ROLE OF ADVOCATE

Much that bears on this topic is simply good apologetics or sound adult education technique. And every clergyman reading thus far has his own equipment—and his church has its own approaches—to utilize at this point in the case. But again at the risk of reciting the obvious I will venture a few suggestions as to approach:

1. *At no point* (role No. 1 or role No. 2) *should the impression be given that it doesn't matter what people believe.* We should not let the couple identify our willingness—even eagerness—that the couple study both sides (or more sides for that matter) with *religious indifferentism,* which is quite

another thing. Especially as the second phase is entered it is important to clarify this point and make it clear that you are now prepared to present the claims of your own tradition with conviction. I do not need to convince Roman Catholic clergy readers of this point. But Roman Catholics all too readily assume that others are not prepared to make a positive case for their Churches—and fault them for it. This point can be answered by doing it!

2. *Do not hesitate to be an advocate.* It is true that apologetically the Roman Catholic priest seems in a stronger position because he can take the clean-cut line that his is the only true Church. Very few non-Roman bodies are prepared to make this claim for themselves. But a Presbyterian minister, for example, is certainly within his heritage to claim that the gospel is more loyally adhered to in his tradition than in the Roman form of Christianity, and an Episcopal priest is being consistent with the Anglican heritage when he says that his tradition is more loyal to the Catholic faith because it is reformed. In so doing neither clergyman is denying that much truth is held by the Roman Catholic Church and by the other Churches too. The reasoned support of particular positions is not vitiated by the fact that it argues toward the conclusion that a given allegiance will be the *best* for the couple and the children because it is the *truest,* rather than toward the conclusion that it is the only true allegiance under Heaven.

3. *Don't get bogged down in minor points.* Since the couple may tend to center on the smaller subjects of their prejudices, it is better for the clergyman to "carry the ball" for the first part of the discussion. He should begin by laying out a bold outline of his church's nature and teaching, with particular reference to major points of difference.[1] It is hoped that the reading which he will be in a position to recommend will do the same.

[1] As a sample, the author will be glad to send any reader requesting it an outline which he has prepared re his own tradition.

4. *Be fair to the end.* There is one point at which there should be a carry-over between the first role and the second: the objectivity and openness characteristic of the referee should come into play as controversial points are being discussed. Sometimes the counselee of his own persuasion will outdistance him—and the truth—in advocacy. Here he will commend himself to the other party—and to the God of truth —by intervening.

> *Case 45.* "But doesn't the Roman Catholic Church teach that Christ is sacrificed over again at each Mass?" said Walter, a Baptist. "No, Walter," answered the Rev. Mr. Simpson, Walter's minister, "one can't say that. While popular teaching and devotional practice often accept this idea, the Church has never officially declared such a position and in fact some of the better minds in the Roman Catholic Church are concerned that such an idea be corrected." Mary, a somewhat unreflective Roman Catholic, who had been unable to answer that taunt when Walter had used it before, was grateful.

Also the clergyman should be alert to see that the counselees are doing adequate reading—on the other side no less than on his own. A suggestion that another volume than the one which they are reading would more adequately present the other position will, we can be sure, be received with good grace.

All of this is particularly important on the part of representatives of traditions which make much of intellectual honesty and freedom of inquiry and really mean it when they affirm that the God of the Church is also the God of truth. Showing this forth in practice is not only good counseling; it is good apologetics.

5. *Don't accept too easy a victory.* Any persuasiveness you and your coreligionist counselee have is all to the good in the cause, but don't allow the other party to sell his own tradition

short. Such is a victory which may prove expensive in the end. Unless you are relatively sure that the change-over is based on sound conviction it is better to hold things up until you are sure that enough reading, talking and thinking have been done.

6. *Encourage questions.* In answering them try to avoid answers which too easily meet the verbalization of the question without meeting the real difficulty. Find as much common ground as you can; concede as much as you can. Distinguish between your own opinions and what your Church officially holds: there may be many matters on which your church has no official position. Say so—and show (if it can be shown) that answers to such questions are not essential to saving faith. If you have a view on it, label it as your own, and use this distinction as an illustration of the freedom of opinion the given tradition permits—if it does.

7. *Talk to both parties at once.* It may be that your first contact with the situation will be through only one of the parties or through a parent or friend of one of them. A first interview with one only should be brief and should be used to accomplish four things:

a. To point up the matter of loyalty and underline the seriousness of the issue enough to avoid a simple capitulation to what may be an imperious approach on the part of the other tradition.

b. To outline the approach you will use in conferences with the two of them—which will be reassuring to your party, and—when passed on—even more so to the other party.

c. To offer genuine hope of a sound solution.

d. To arrange a time for a fuller conference with both.

But the main work should be done with both present, so that there will be a maximum of confidence on the part of the "outsider."

CLOSING STEPS

The remaining phases of the relationship depend of course upon the outcome of the couple's deliberations.

If they have both decided upon another tradition, assure yourself that they have considered all aspects and if they feel they have, wish them well—with good grace, assuring them that your door is always open to them should doubts or questions later enter their minds.

If they are still disparate religiously, usually they should be advised not to marry (unless there is some compelling reason for them to go ahead). If they nevertheless will, then, as pastor, you should remind your party of his obligations as to the religious nurture of the children and hope he will stand as firmly as the other party on this issue—and thus on the issue as to the forum for the marriage. If your party nevertheless gives in, remind him that no arrangements made in connection with the marriage release him of his primary ethical obligation to bring into the lives of the children the best religious heritage he knows (see Chapter X).

If they have decided upon your tradition, then the principal task left (other than arranging the marriage itself) is to help the couple meet the reactions of the converted party's parents and relatives. As suggested above, this may not turn out to be so devastating a problem as it first seems. What appears from a distance to be too steep a grade generally levels out when you ascend it. Whether it should or not, love of kith and kin often prevails over the strictures of even the most exclusivist traditions. But it is of course true that in some cases the convert really becomes—and remains—an outcast. Here we simply have to count on the combined weight of the religious fervor of a convert and devotion to his spouse-to-be— generally a pretty forceful combination. But a permanent exclusion from the life of one of the two families should never be accepted as an irreversible fact, and the strength of the deepening of the religious basis of the couple's new-found life should provide resources for the constant holding forth of love and interest, even if at first it seems unreciprocated, or even rebuffed. Experience teaches that generally one, or perhaps both, of the parents will end up coming to the wedding; and, in the months which follow, the sincere religious devotion of the two can hardly be brushed aside by even the most dogmatic. And in due time the appearance of a grandchild is a pretty effective melter of hearts.

If in breaking the news the couple reveals the process gone through leading to the decision, and if—without stirring up arguments—the reason for the change is cast in terms of the appeal to truth and not as a personal concession, it is more difficult for the parents to revert to the emotional labels discussed earlier. And the continued witness to the faith held, in sweet-tempered and intelligent conversation (when it seems relevant in the course of everyday relationships), may do more than one dare hope for. It may even strengthen the faith of the parents in the great verities held in common. It may even move them to rethink their own religious position. It has happened.

INDEX

72 73 74 75 10 9 8

IF YOU MARRY OUTSIDE YOUR FAITH

Counsel on Mixed Marriages

Revised Edition

BY JAMES A. PIKE

"This is a remarkable book by a remarkable man. It is the first full-length treatment, from the Protestant side, of the thorny question of marriages between persons of different religious loyalties. It examines the whole subject from the standpoint both of basic principles and of practical procedures." —*Religious Book Club Bulletin*

"Here is a book not only for persons contemplating a mixed marriage, but for all concerned with counseling— clergy, social workers, and the general reader." —*The Living Church*

"This book should be read by every young person long before he or she contemplates marriage. The heartaches and tragedies of the mixed marriage, which all ministers know, will be greatly reduced if this volume gets a wide reading." —*The Pulpit*

HARPER & ROW, PUBLISHERS

the time, and which, if he understands the meaning of his Protestant faith, may become an intolerable one. Many pastors know of the agony through which some of their members have gone as a result. It is an open question whether one is morally obligated to keep a vow which one has made under a type of duress, and which comes to be regarded as contrary to the religious conscience. . . . [Here follows a discussion of legal aspects of the antenuptial agreement. See Chapter V.][17]

REFORMED

There is no synodical resolution of the Reformed Church in America, but the matter is covered in a pamphlet on family counseling issued by the Church's Christian Action Commission.[18]

UNITED CHURCH OF CANADA

It is recommended that:

(1) The United Church of Canada re-affirm the historic position of the Christian Church in discouraging mixed marriages, in principle:

(2) Our ministers counsel young people who contemplate contracting a mixed marriage to refuse to sign any document that would alienate their right to be spiritual guides to their own children or that would reflect on the validity of their own church membership;

(3) The Federal Council of Churches pamphlet entitled, "If I Marry a Roman Catholic," be put in the hands of any United Church member contemplating a mixed marriage.

(4) The Commission on the Christian Faith be requested to prepare a manual of Protestant doctrine, including a declaration of belief, for the use of Roman Catholics who intend to marry Protestants.[19]

UNITED CHURCH OF CHRIST

The Church of Jesus Christ has the solemn responsibility to teach each new generation God's holy purpose for marriage, to estab-

[17] Minutes of the General Assembly, Presbyterian Church, U.S., 1948, p. 160(2).
[18] 475 Riverside Drive, New York 27, N.Y.
[19] Record of Proceedings, General Council, United Church of Canada, Montreal, 1946, p. 145.

lish the conditions so far as possible for its realization, and to warn against the dangers which threaten it. That purpose has been clearly disclosed in the words of our Lord: "From the beginning of creation, 'God made them male and female.' 'For this reason a man shall leave his father and mother and be joined to his wife, and the two shall become one.' So they are no longer two but one. What therefore God has joined together, let no man put asunder" (Mark 10:6–9).

The Apostle Paul has affirmed the sanctity and defined the character of the union of man and wife by comparing that union to the relation of Christ and his church: "Husbands, love your wives, as Christ loved the church and gave himself up for her. . . . For no man ever hates his own flesh, but nourishes and cherishes it, as Christ does the church, because we are members of his body" (Ephesians 5:25, 29 f.).

It is abundantly clear that the realization of God's purpose for married life—like every relation of Christian people to each other and to their fellow men—is grounded in and sustained by a sincere faith in God and a constant devotion to Christ and his church. The marriage relation is strengthened and sanctified when both man and wife meet the joys and sorrows, the stresses and strains, the successes and disappointments of their lives with a shared Christian faith and worship.

Marriages between Christians and non-Christians, therefore, present obvious obstacles to the realization in marriage of the full purpose of God. Even marriage between Protestant and Roman Catholic Christians involves difficulties arising out of different and partly incompatible interpretations of Christian truth. Because such a marriage puts obstacles in the way of realizing a union that can be compared to the union of Christ and his church, we call attention to the problems involved.

Both the Roman Catholic and the Protestant churches have been aware that difficulties exist. The Roman Church has devised and used an "antenuptial contract" as one means of dealing with so-called "mixed marriages"—marriages between a Roman Catholic and a non-Roman Catholic. Protestant churches have avoided the use of such a device as something alien to the character of Protestantism.

The marriage of a Roman Catholic to a Protestant Christian

often involves grave spiritual hardship for one partner or for both and for their children as well. The Roman Catholic Christian has been taught to believe that the Roman Catholic Church alone is the true Church of Christ; that its dogmas have the character of infallible truth; that marriage is a sacrament and that the grace of Christ is bestowed on the couple only as marriage is solemnized by a priest of the Roman Catholic Church.

The Protestant Christian believes that the Word of God as disclosed in the Old and New Testaments is the rule of faith and practice and that the church is *under* that Word of God. He believes that many of the dogmatic positions of the Roman Church—such as, its dogmas concerning man, grace, sacraments, and the Virgin—are not consistent with biblical teaching. For the Protestant, Christian marriage is not a sacrament but a solemn rite, performed by the church. Its validity and rightness in God's providence is established by a free response of both parties to God's will as revealed in His word. For the Protestant, marriage is a holy and honorable estate, not a concession to human weakness. For the Protestant, the whole of life is lived in dependence on the grace of God in Christ given wholly and directly to those who put their trust and confidence in Him. Marriage does not require a special grace mediated only through a priesthood to make it acceptable to God.

The Roman Catholic Church requires every member to accept its authority in all matters of faith and imposes its discipline upon those who disobey. The Protestant church member, on the other hand, enjoys the freedom of a child of God under the guidance of the Holy Spirit and the Word.

All of these differences make for difficulties. The Roman Catholic is confronted by the choice, either of alienating himself from his church by being married by a Protestant minister or of persuading the other party to the marriage to submit to being married by a Roman Catholic priest. In the latter case, the Protestant party is asked to acknowledge that his church is not truly a church of Christ, that his beliefs are in error, and that the marriage is valid only if performed by a Roman Catholic priest.

Such agreements can hardly fail to produce a void, if not a rift, at the very center of spiritual life in the family, not only between husband and wife but also between the parents and the children. The consequences are frequently not limited to parents and children, but extend to the wider circles of the family. If religious faith in both partners is sincere and strong, as it should be, there can scarcely be the same warmth and fullness of kinship as when there is a mutual respect for sincerely held convictions or when both are of the same faith.

In mixed marriages, the claim of the Roman Catholic Church to be the only true church, as implied in the provisions of the antenuptial contract, makes religion a divisive force in the family rather than the greatest bond of unity and allegiance, as intended by Almighty God. Certainly a home in which one party is assumed to be right while the other is assumed to be wrong has a great handicap to overcome in the building of enduring mutual esteem, harmony, and love. Such difficulties help to explain why more than twice as many mixed marriages end in divorce as when both parties are of the same faith.

Protestant Christians will not surrender their faith lightly; and they ought not to do so. They will also do well to ask whether a marriage entered into under the conditions imposed by the Roman Catholic Church provides a sound spiritual basis for happy and successful family life. Unless one himself believes in the Roman Catholic interpretation of Christianity firmly enough to become an honest and sincere adherent of that faith *before* marrying under the conditions prescribed by the Roman Catholic Church, it is wrong to commit one's unborn children to a faith that he cannot wholeheartedly embrace. It is equally wrong to withhold from them the Protestant's freedom and joy of direct access to God.

Protestant Christians need to be on guard against two false ways of escape from the problems raised by mixed marriages. One false way is to take any vow lightly or to subscribe to it with mental reservations. All vows are responsible acts in the sight of God. Taking a vow with the mental reservation that one does not intend to fulfill his promises is dishonest. It does not constitute a "solution" of the difficulties created by the conditions imposed by the Church of Rome.

A second false way is for the parties to a mixed marriage to fall into an attitude of religious indifference. A right relationship with God is the chief end of our lives. It is certainly not attained by indifference to God.